TRUST-BASED

LEADERSHIP

Endorsements

Charles has the ability to bring in unique perspectives, and this book is no exception. It brings out some very critical and not so well appreciated aspects of leadership that are fundamental to inspire teams. These deep insights come from his personal experiences. His sharing of these anecdotes makes the reader connect and comprehend the concepts easily. This book adds a new dimension to our understanding of leadership. It is a must-read book for managers and academics who are looking to inspire and lead in the real world.

Avijit Das, CEO and MD, Eveready Pty Ltd

I was very privileged to have met Charles Du Toit at NMU Business School when he was lecturing the MBA Leadership module. He has since then successfully facilitated several interventions for BKB Ltd across our businesses and departments, where we were exposed to his passion, expertise, practical approach and truly authentic leadership coaching and training. He furthermore played an instrumental role in establishing our in-house leadership academy and collective leadership brand through the nine trust-based principles – a powerful tool indeed for any leader. Highly recommended!

Karen Posthumus, General Manager: Human Resources, BKB Ltd

I have known Charles for many years, all of those in senior leadership positions. He is a champion in the fields of Human Resources as well as the leadership of life. He has had to cope with numerous challenges and handles them with a positive attitude. He is a great guy to help your team in respect of leadership because he has energy, enthusiasm, empathy and is trustworthy. The book is going to give you an insight regarding some principles to guide you and your team. It is Charles' inspirational approach that will really help organisations.

Johnny Goldberg, Chairman, Global Business Solutions

Charles Du Toit has devoted much of his life to the study of leadership. His doctorate in the field is, of course, of great value, but it is his direct experience in leadership positions and in observing and communicating with other leaders in many fields that makes his contribution especially useful. His nine principles are strongly grounded in relationship choices. Communicating complex issues simply is a skill – a leadership skill. In this simply written short book, Charles shares his deep understanding of leadership as a form of influence based on trust, and its critical contribution to shaping organisational culture. Strongly recommended for leaders at all levels across fields and organisational types.

Mark Anstey, Emeritus Professor, Nelson Mandela University

"We first met Charles soon after going through a major change in our business and we were busy configuring an all-new company. This entailed redesigning the leadership team's culture and approach, amongst many other start-up challenges. Charles Du Toit is a unique and gifted person who has that rare combination of industrial and academic experience. He had just the right background to assist us with ensuring that our management team was properly equipped to understand their leadership role and to address the many strategic and business issues we were facing. While Charles has a doctorate in the leadership field, it is his ability to relate to all levels that cements his success. Leadership is as much an art as it is a science; it is not an easy topic to deal with. Charles shares many deep understandings in his book and it will serve as a very useful guide to all those who have been tasked with the leadership mantle.

Billy Tom, President and CEO, Isuzu Motors South Africa

Early in the book, Charles makes the point that "self-reflection is the most important leadership tool". In many respects, this contribution to the conversation and debate on leadership is precisely that – the reflections of Charles about his lived experience of leadership. This also positions the book in terms of potential audience. This is not an "academic" book, but a simply written exploration of what your personal leadership brand may mean and how it could be developed. It is therefore specifically of potential value to emerging leaders or people who are participating in formal leadership development processes. Given the post-pandemic phase we are in, namely to explore, discover and develop new approaches to leadership, the usefulness of this book is not in the answers it provides, but in the questions it raises in the mind of the reader. In this way, it will serve the purpose of stimulating mindful and purposeful self-reflection.

Dr Anton Verwey, Executive Strategy and Innovation, inavitiQ (Pty) Ltd

My leadership journey started in 2015 when I led two employees without any formal leadership training. As I further matured into the organisation in 2019, I started a leadership course with Dr Charles Du Toit. Charles helped me to formulate a bridge between what I thought leadership meant and its reality, transforming and deepening my thinking on leadership tools and their application. I have learnt that leadership is less about self and almost entirely about others. This defines who we ought to become – selfless leaders.

Within his methods of building leadership muscle, we created a leadership brand statement that has helped me formulate the basis of who I want to become both personally and professionally. This has become my leadership DNA since 2019 and I have not looked back.

Alone is faster, together is further! Are you ready for your enriching journey?

Mr. Zafar Sain, National Key Account Manager, BestDrive, Continental Tyre SA (Pty) Ltd

I will be using this 'little book' a lot, both to assist me with making my own leadership choices, as well as to support and coach others to make theirs. The focus on nine principles and the reflection exercises simplifies a huge topic often associated with charismatic characters, into something that is possible for each of us to achieve. I really love how Charles shares anecdotes, making his leadership journey personal and relatable. The leader's responsibility to build relationships outside of their comfort zone is at the core of our future leadership challenges as we embrace diversity in the workplace.

Cathy Albertyn, Group People & Culture Officer, Coa-Cola Beverages Africa

Dr Charles Du Toit hits the nail on the head when he says leadership is a choice and a calling. He describes how leader build trust and influence though deliberately connecting with our teams. This form of leadership leads to high performance organisations. This brand of leadership will do this for your organisation.

Bobby Stephenson, Member of the East Province Legislature

First published in 2022.

ISBN: 978-1-86922-960-3 (Printed)
eISBN: 978-1-86922-961-0 (PDF eBook)

Published by KR Publishing
Republic of South Africa
Tel: (011) 706-6009
E-mail: orders@knowres.co.za
Website: www.kr.co.za

Typesetting, layout and design: Cia Joubert, cia@knowres.co.za
Cover design: Marlene de'Lorme, marlene@knowres.co.za
Artwork: Charles Du Toit
Editing and proofreading: Jennifer Renton, jenniferrenton@live.co.za
Project management: Cia Joubert, cia@knowres.co.za

TRUST-BASED

LEADERSHIP

THE 9 PRINCIPLES

DR CHARLES DU TOIT

kr
publishing

2022

Dedication

This book is dedicated to Ingrid.

Luv, you are the inspiration. You gave me the courage to do things differently and the confidence to share without fear.

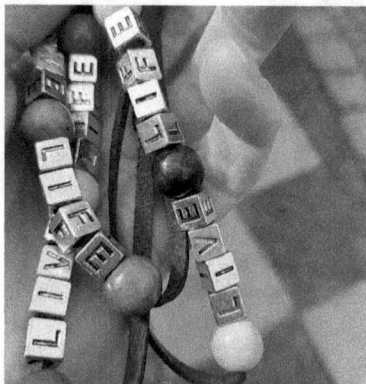

I miss you beyond words. You continue to inspire my spirit.

Live Life.

Acknowledgements

I would like to thank the following people:

- Wilhelm Crous for your belief in this project and for his support on my journey.

- Cia for patiently knitting the book together.

- Janine Roe for the huge job editing this dyslexic

- Noeline my business partner for holding everything together

- My son Ian for his support and encouragement

- Tanya for all the encouragement.

Table of Contents

About the Author

Dr Charles Du Toit achieved a PHD in leadership from the University of Johannesburg in 2014 and *"The role of HR in creating a leadership brand"* has defined his current mission.

Dr Du Toit spent 14 years at VWSA in various IR, HR and training leadership roles. He also served as the HR Director at Eveready (PTY) Ltd for 15 years and HR Executive at MA Automotive for a year.

Dr Du Toit now leads his own consultancy, Dr Charles Du Toit and Associates, which focuses on Leadership, Business, Human Resources and Conflict Management – coaching, teaching and facilitating both academic and corporate clients.

He further lectures leadership and HR subjects at the master's and Doctoral levels for NMMU, Stellenbosch and TUT universities, and regularly publishes topical leadership articles. He has published a book and is currently working on his second book on Leadership.

Dr Du Toit's community roles have included being member of NMMU Business School's advisory board, Chair of the Nelson Mandela Bay HR Forum, founder and Chair of the Uitenhage Peace Committee and SGB Chair of the Quest School for Autism.

Dr Du Toit offers specialised one-on-one and group coaching sessions that build on learning experiences with facilitated reflection. His coaching programme, which is for new and existing leaders, is designed around specific needs and issues identified in close consultation with the employee(s). During these sessions, structured guidance and critical insight are provided that promote positive leadership growth.

Charles Du Toit and Associates products include:

- bespoke corporate and individual leadership brand development programs,
- corporate leadership academies,
- two full year SETA certified leadership learnerships at entry and advanced levels and
- one-on-one and group coaching sessions.

During all these interventions Dr du Toit provides leaders with a dynamic experience of guidance, reflection and critical insight that promote positive trust-based leadership growth.

Preface

"I don't have time for another simplistic model of leadership." This was the comment by an executive manager participating in one of my programmes. I was told she was just having a bad day, but her unsolicited statement threw me somewhat. In hindsight, I think I could have countered with the question, "Do you think a complex model would be more useful?"

You see, I have waded through a massive amount of "complex" leadership theory. While this is academically interesting, presents well in business schools and sells books, it is not especially useful if you are not an academic but rather a business or professional person striving to lead in a competitive, high-pressure world.

That is the world I live in, and why this book is written in a "non-academic" style. (I have included a light overview of leadership theory at the back of this book to show you how what I am arguing lands within leadership theory, but we'll leave that for last.)

To build on these principles, I prefer simplicity in terms of language and logic to help you relate to your own life experience and reflection. Each chapter is a logical step that you will find organically leads to the next. I believe that you will find this book to be an easy read. Its purpose and intent are to take you on a journey that will provide you with insights and principles which can ultimately constructively guide your life as a leader.

MY DEEPEST HOPE IS THAT THIS BOOK PROVIDES YOU WITH THE TOOLS TO LEAD MINDFULLY, MEANINGFULLY AND AUTHENTICALLY. MAY YOUR RELATIONSHIP-BASED LEADERSHIP EXPERIENCE GIVE YOU THE SAME JOY AND FULFILMENT IT HAS GIVEN ME AND MANY OTHERS WHO HAVE APPLIED THESE SIMPLE PRINCIPLES.

Why have I focused on these specific but incredibly simple principles?

I believe you will find that I make no fanciful claims in the material discussed here. I am fully and humbly aware that many more similar principles are out there, but to build a simple and healthy foundation I resolved to work with these nine principles for now. My experience in working with approximately 2,000 leaders has affirmed over and over for me and those I have coached, that these elementary principles work and fit together. Many of the well-known leadership models I have come across explain different characteristics or features of leadership in what may present as a cluster, with links connecting the various elements. I contend that *leadership is first and foremost, a relationship,* and the linked concepts are less Sherlock Holmes and more common sense.

The nine principles presented in this book follow in logical sequence, and my intent is to build a clear picture of what leadership can potentially be at its very core. This core translates into "the leadership relationship". The balance of other leadership characteristics is, of course, important, and evolve within each of us as leaders in line with our own personality and environment. What is significant and what I have continuously experienced in practice, is that without the key leadership **relationship**, other characteristics and traits have been known to translate to being somewhat more opportunistic than based on leadership influence. I will review why I say this as we navigate through the fundamentals.

In the middle of Covid-19, I printed out a first draft of this book. On reflection I felt that it was somewhat okay. It contained technically correct references and was peppered with anecdotal stories from my personal experience around leadership principles. I had gotten to re-reading up to about 160 pages, but at this point I decided that what I had written thus far paralleled a myriad of other books I had read on leadership and that wasn't what I was aiming for. So, I tossed the draft and went back to the drawing board.

I have reflected on, read, researched, interviewed and taught leadership practice as an exclusive topic for 10 years now; it has become my life's work and passion. The result is a desire to be able to present an uncomplicated understanding of leadership. Not because it needs to be such, for publication purposes, but because I really am convinced that leadership is this simple. I honestly believe that there is no value in making the principles embodied herein overly complex. In this high pressure environment I understand that your time is a precious commodity.

This book is created with you, the business, public servant or societal leader in mind. I appreciate that for you to find the time and space to read a leadership book is challenging, so I have tried to make it straightforward, logical and succinct.

On a flight to Johannesburg

I was on a flight to Johannesburg from Cape Town. This was in the pre-Covid-19 days and flying was a way of life. Next to me sat a very well-dressed man, who greeted me quite formally when I sat down. He asked me where I grew up and when I told him that I was born in Port Elizabeth, he immediately warmed to me and began telling me of his childhood in New Brighton where he was raised by his grandmother.

He asked me what my line of business was, and I explained that I teach leadership development as a profession. "Wow", he replied, "that is fascinating, and so important today". I likewise probed him on his line of work and learned that he was a policeman. He then asked me to explain what leadership really meant. He seemed very keen to learn more, so I put away my earphones and we started a conversation.

He literally squeezed the nine principles I teach in this book out of me, step for step, question by question. While I had been teaching these principles for a long time, there was to me, a beauty in this simple step-by-step approach. He would ask a question, listen carefully to my answers, and then test my answer against his lived experience. As we spoke, I gradually took him through these simple principles. Each one logical and simple in concept, but infinitely more challenging in practice. I could see as we talked how his understanding began to take shape – an understanding beyond mere theory but rather a resonating of personal conviction.

The one-and-a-half-hour flight went by very quickly.

By the time we reached Johannesburg I had gleaned two things about my flight companion. Firstly, he was not a rank-and-file policeman, but held a very senior position as Brigadier General for the province. Secondly, he presented as being very humble and despite his senior position, remarkably he had never really explored the dynamics of, or properly understood, leadership up to this point.

The following questions he asked form the outline of this book.

1.   Which theory of leadership did I support? Leadership is not a 'one-size-fits-all theory' – it is a choice.

2.   So, what is leadership really? Leadership is first a relationship.

3. How does this work in practice? Relationships are about connection and trust.

4. Are we not all responsible for our relationships in any event? So, what is so special about a leadership relationship? In a leadership relationship the leader is responsible for the relationship.

5. How do we build leadership relationships, with all the noise around business deliverables? Leaders build trust through switching off autopilot and deliberately connecting.

6. But life it is not so simple; people can be challenging and what about leading when things go wrong? Leadership "moments" amplify the connection/trust experience.

7. So why is this trust so important? Trust is not a thing but a consequence. Trust is the consequence of the experience of the other over time. In leadership, the by-product of trust for leaders is influence.

8. What if this 'connection stuff' is just not who I am? What are the alternatives? The alternative to leadership influence is to command and evoke fear.

9. How does your leadership style affect the organisation? An organisation's culture is the reflection of the organisation's leadership and how they lead.

10. Why does this sound so different from what we were led to believe? Today, followers are more than just assets – they can be the source of competitive advantage.

The idea of this book is for you and me to take a journey together, just like the Brigadier-General and I; to sit down and share ideas and then to unpack them.

I have included a Visual Memory page in each chapter because I have found that our visual memories are able to retain information for longer and more effectively than our auditory ones.

In this exploration of nine fundamental principles, I have included a brief overview of the past, as well as the potential future of, leadership trends.

I sincerely hope that you find this simple format, whilst it may deviate from the norm, to be of great personal benefit. I am confident that when you apply these principles, you will discover for yourself the real joy of leading in the modern context.

I recommend that while reading the chapters you bear the following in mind:

- Critically examine the principles presented against your lived experience.

- Self-reflection is the most important leadership tool.

- Consider your own teams in their unique context and how you think they may respond to the application of each of the principles in this book.

- Do not be afraid to make notes in the book or use a journal in conjunction with it.

- As you work with the input from this book, other leadership theories, and observe the world around you, I recommend that you begin to develop your personal leadership brand.

- Most importantly, if you take on board an idea or principle, it is key that you create a personal discipline so that with time, this principle becomes second nature.

Thoughts on Developing your own Leadership Brand

With the plethora of theories and publications available around Leadership Branding, it can be fairly daunting and confusing to decide which would be a natural fit, as there is no 'one-size-fits-all' model or solution. The challenge is therefore to find your "unique style which fits in with your persona".

"As a leader, you begin to build a public brand, whether you like it or not. People will develop an opinion and your behaviour and style will reinforce it over time."[1] Leaving it to chance is not sustainable. Here are a few pointers to guide you in the right direction.

1. **Become leadership aware**

    a. Read all you can about leadership.

    b. Take note, observe the multiple leadership lessons going on around you daily, and try to identify the leadership component as you read the paper, attend a meeting or even watch a sports match.

    c. Observe closely how others respond to your leadership.

2. *Develop an opinion*

   As you apply and practice your leadership, you will begin to recognise what works for you and what does not, what inspires you and what does not, and how subordinates responded when you did things a certain way.

3. *Journal or record your experiences and observations*

   Make it a daily habit and learn from your notes.

4. *Constantly refresh and recalibrate*

   Developing a leadership brand is a lifelong discipline. Your personal brand needs constant reflection and recalibration.

Find a system that will work for you, but make it a matter of intent and mindfulness. For more on the topic, visit:

> https://charlesdutoit.co.za/2017/12/09/the-immeasurable-value-of-discovering-your-personal-leadership-brand/

Years ago, I was given an exciting coaching assignment. A very dynamic, authentic woman had been promoted to a senior position within the Sales Division of a well-known automotive brand. She had attended my 'Discover your Personal Leadership Brand' programme and had asked for me to be her transitional coach as she prepared to move up to the new challenge. We journeyed through these principles together and at each stage she reflected upon how this would translate directly into her new role. This process of careful reflection produced a spectacular result. I have included the tools which emerged from this reflective process after each chapter for your own consideration as a workbook exercise.

I would also recommend that you return to the following exercise after each chapter to cement and consolidate what you are gleaning from the material.

Activity 1

Chapter	1	2	3	4	5	6	7	8	9	10
1. Have you critically examined the ideas presented against your lived experience?										
2. Did you reflect on the tools and ideas of the section?										
3. Consider your team. How will they respond to you with key ideas?										
4. Did you make notes in the book, or use a journal?										
5. Do you have a simple tool with which you can practice each process to ensure that over time this concept or truth becomes habit?										

PART 1

When I started writing this manuscript, I was very inspired to write an accessible, non-academic, reflective guide to trust-based leadership.

This ambition, however, had a drawback, as it could be argued that what I have written has no academic or research grounding. I am passionate about the practice of leadership and have dedicated a significant part of my life to studying the various leadership theories and this has influenced every reflection or principle. The solution was to craft a book in two parts.

Part 1 of this book is designed to journey with you through nine key principles underpinning Trust-based leadership. I do this in what I hope is a unique and practical way, reflecting with you on how they can work in practice.

CHAPTER 1

Principle 1: Leadership is more than a one-size-fits-all theory or a personality type; leadership is a choice

Why describe leadership as a lived experience and choice as opposed to a theory? As a teacher in the field of leadership, I am very conscious of how important this distinction is. Like most topics that have a lot of theories underlining them, it is possible to understand leadership theoretically, and yet not put it into practice at all. Unlike other business disciplines, leadership practice is not system or process driven. Leadership is what a manager, a coach, a police captain or a director does when they arrive at the office, sports field, station, board room or any of the other myriad leadership contexts.

This differentiation was illustrated to me in a unique way at the South African National HR Directors conference a year ago. I was privileged to lead an expert workshop with an associate of mine on the theme of "Employee Engagement and Culture".

The room was filled with high flying executive HR Director types, all reasonably confident in their own experience and knowledge. While some of the participants were there to learn and share ideas, I got the distinct impression that some were there to grandstand. In the middle of the workshop a particularly 'confident' young colleague played the proverbial 'business school' leadership card.

"So, tell me," he challenged with a somewhat cynical look on his face (his thought bubble implying, 'if you are so clever'), "are leaders born or are they created?"

"Do you drink wine?" I asked him. He looked at me with as if to say "Really?" and responded to his now captive audience, "Yes. I am a wine connoisseur".

"Great!" I replied. "Your question is a bit like asking someone if the wine they're sampling is red or white, and the obvious answer of course is that wine can be either red or white. While the many diverse wines taste different, come from different regions, fruit varietals, age differently and all appeal to different palates, wine is essentially wine."

I could quickly see that this simple analogy was not impressing the young business school wine connoisseur. I wanted to keep him engaged and interested, so I probed some more.

"Is wine made from grapes or apples?" I asked. "From grapes of course!", he retorted whilst looking around at the others and rolling his eyes with simulated irritation.

"So, we agree that wine can be either red or white", I ventured, "but it will always be made from grapes". He concurred reluctantly.

"This is the point", I explained, "beyond your *born* or *created* question, there is a further key ingredient which, if missing, will make either or both concepts irrelevant".

"Let me explain", I continued. "The tricky part of the 'leaders – born or made' that I question, is that the answer could be 'neither, either or both'. But I believe this is the wrong question to start with. I feel strongly that when you are speaking about leadership, the question around being "born" or "created" is irrelevant. Just as red or white wine is wine, 'wine' made from other fruit may be similar in appearance and colour to wine made from grapes, but it is not wine."

Let's scrutinise the two options a little more closely.

"If you argue that leaders are **born**", I explained, "life will probably have revealed to you by now that there are a host of highly effective leaders who do not fit the classic 'Great Man' leader profile. Life will also have shown you that there are a multitude of people who display the typical 'Alpha' Great Man traits or characteristics, but who are to all intents and purposes terrible managers".

I expanded, "This does not mean that our genetics do not influence our ability to lead. Think about some of the executives you have met. I don't know about you, but when I contemplate the scope of their functions and the range of relationships and processes which they need to keep a beady eye on, I am awed".

"Some have a genetic capacity which allows them to cope with serious complexity and consequently when they are promoted to higher levels, they are very comfortable with the complexities inherent in the next job level. Of course, we know the converse is true, as there are many examples of promotions where people do not cope so well." (We call this effect the Peter Principle, or 'stratified systems theory'.)

''If you answered that leaders are **made**", I continued, "this almost presupposes that anyone can lead. Leadership "**making**" can sound almost like simply taking a tablet, following a formula, or going to the gym to shape up. This is an over-simplification, implying that managers merely need to be provided with plenty of the appropriate tools and that therefore basically anybody can pull off being a leader".

"Can anyone improve on their leadership ability, with insight and good leadership education?", I asked. "I must believe this", I continued, "as my entire practice assumes that this is indeed possible. I would argue that good leadership training, like any skill, can certainly make a difference". It is also possible that a manager may attend a significant leadership development programme but never embrace a personal leadership brand.

"We will argue that authentic leadership only emerges through personal reflection and insight. This practice transcends both born (genetic) and made (developed) leadership capabilities."

I will show in this book, however, that the real answer to the question of whether leaders are born or made is that both our genetics and our training will influence the type of leader we become, but neither of these elements necessarily guarantee that we will lead effectively.

I am convinced that leadership needs to be more than a theory, a learnt skill or a genetic predisposition.

Leadership is a choice...

"Without making the intentional choice to lead, it is possible that neither our genetic makeup, nor our level of education will be of any relevance", I continued. "However, once we actively decide to lead, then our genetic capabilities as well our skills and/or understanding of leadership concepts will enhance and influence the type of leadership we express."

As I explained these concepts, I observed how the entire audience was feverishly making notes. I knew that I had hit a nerve. Then hands went up. "Which choice?" "How do leaders make this choice to lead?" "How do we train leaders this way?"

The business school wine connoisseur looked up and grinned at me in silent acknowledgement, as if to say, "They didn't teach me *that*".

Making Leadership Real

Go into any bookshop and you will find a whole section of books on leadership, some of which are significant works and some of which are similar in size to this book. Each of these books presents a series of laws or leadership principles which then tend to become those 'in vogue' ideas thrown around in the board room. We also find anecdotal books – the biographies of famous people and how they came to leadership. Leaders ranging from celebrity sportspeople to great CEOs and political leaders have published books on this subject. Some of these you may be familiar with across a wide spectrum, from Jack Welsh to Richard Branson, Graham Smith to Keith Christy, Nelson Mandela to Rudi Giuliani, and Barack Obama and Hitler to Churchill.

For the regular supervisor, team or line leader, division head or company owner, however, these books authored by famous people and their complex theories are often worlds apart from their daily experiences. Leaders such as the police station commander, the school principal and the hundreds of leaders who lead within organisations have a direct impact on their people and their organisations. It goes without saying that there would be a significantly positive impact if they lead well, and conversely, a negative impact if they lead poorly.

I personally find this dynamic extremely challenging. Other fields such as management, finance, production and project management have a reasonably standard, concrete set of rules and principles, which guide practice. At business schools across the world, however, we have been studying leadership for years, but we have yet to fully manage getting leadership nailed down to an exact formula.

In the field of leadership, it is noteworthy that the more I researched, the more divergent were the theories I came across. What I found even more frustrating was that each divergent theory had some or other body of research supporting the theorist's claim that his/her approach provides 'superior' insight.

When we look at leadership as simply a theory, we are probably already missing the point. Leadership theory may be of interest or value to social scientists and academics, but for a young businessperson, or someone who is leading a team of employees, leadership is a daily challenge and often the most difficult part of the job.

I PREFER TO SEE LEADERSHIP AS A PERSONAL CALLING AND A CHOICE AS OPPOSED TO A THEORY!

I believe that leadership is a choice, or as we discussed earlier on, a *decision*, and *not simply a process*. Whereas management processes can be written up as Standard Operating Procedures and we can develop measurement tools and assess compliance, it is not so for leadership.

While in the past there have been attempts to put leadership into a 'standard box', measuring and recognising leadership styles by output, I am convinced that the aspirant modern leader should be recognised as a competent leader, not by the theory he or she ascribes to, nor purely by the output achieved. It is rather the input – the ability to influence and create an environment where followers thrive – where real modern leadership is measured. This is the true litmus test.

Let me illustrate...

I found that one of the greatest challenges I had to deal with as an HR executive was concerning management who were excellent individual contributors but had not definitively made the decision to lead. A classic case was Anna.

Anna was an experienced logistics manager who was exceptionally good at her job. She had strong global networks, a deep insight into the MRP (the IT production planning system) and an excellent work ethic. She took personal responsibility for the build plan, which was highly complex and required her very specific skills set. The senior management team relied upon her insight and good judgement, so she gained their respect on that score. Initially she would shoot the lights out on deliverables and consistently exceeded her KPIs.

But as time went by, our organisation increasingly began focusing on the culture and the quality of the organisation's leadership. While KPIs and results were still non-negotiable, we began to take notice of the management input aspect of getting a job done. One of the tools we implemented to ensure that we lived up to the values the company signed up for was a 360° leadership assessment.

Anna started coming to the attention of senior management as a problem. She was responsible for 12 people who 'suffered' under her leadership. She was a decidedly unpleasant and moody person. She could be extremely rude to anyone whom she felt was not at her level and had a brutal and sarcastic manner. She was also prone to radical mood swings.

As my office was down the passage from her, I could tell what kind of day her staff were going to have just by listening to the sound of her heels on the tiles as she walked past my office in the morning. The younger employees in the division were particularly afraid of her, and for good reason. She could be extremely cutting, which made them feel invalidated and devalued. Staff turnover was high, but no one dared complain publicly for fear of incurring her wrath.

But then came the 360° results and Anna 'bombed big-time'. That's when I got involved and began a coaching and counselling process with her. Sadly, Anna could not see the problem. In her mind she was the hero and needed to hear that constantly. Her results (deliverables) were still excellent but now she was being measured on a different level and was failing badly.

No measure of coaching would help her as she just could or would not accept that while she was achieving great results on one level, this was not all she was employed to do. Her job required that she manage a team of people, and she just could not access the human element of the passion to lead; the passion for her team.

Sadly, after a six month intervention she threw in the towel. She accused the organisation of under-appreciating her and resigned.

The change in her department was gradual. The members of the team initially felt so disempowered that they would hang back and not contribute meaningfully at all. Thankfully though, they slowly began to discover their own voices and an entirely different departmental culture emerged which previously had been patently missing.

After about six months the logistics team became so effective internally that we never did replace Anna. Instead of one achievement-focused, driven but grumpy employee and a set of slaves, we found that we had a team of logistics experts who were dynamic and innovative. Another surprising spin-off was that the seemingly complex build planning process turned out to be much simpler than previously imagined.

As you can see in the case of Anna, it is not impossible to achieve business results where a leader lacks commitment to the team and the human element. However, in the modern context, this is perhaps not good enough (even though our team may be enthused), nor should it be acceptable. When we inspire our teams, individually and collectively, they are most likely to perform at their optimum. This speaks into the choice placed before modern leadership and is the case I am building is for trust-based leadership. This was beautifully described by Admiral Grace Hooper, the first female admiral in the US Navy in the 1970s:

"YOU MANAGE THINGS, YOU LEAD PEOPLE!"

Two sides of a coin...

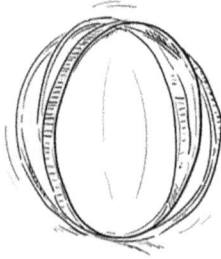

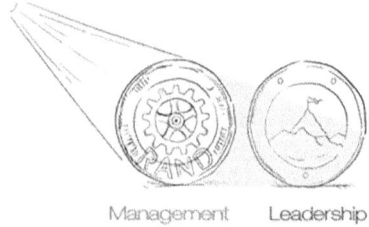

Management   Leadership

In this first chapter I have argued that whether he or she is a born, made or some blend of both leader, a manager only really becomes a leader when he or she *decides* to lead.

Merriam Webster's definition of the word "choice" is: "the opportunity or power to choose between two or more possibilities: the opportunity or power to make a decision." This implies that it lies within your scope and power as a leader to decide which way you will choose. In context you are ultimately the one who must choose to take up the challenge to lead authentically and with commitment, consistently and continuously. Choose to develop your own passion to lead! This is precisely why I talk about leadership not as a theory, but as a choice.

Reflection Exercise

Principle 1: Leadership is not a one-size-fits-all theory, it is a choice!

Which side of the 'are leaders born or made' debate do you find yourself on and why?

Does the concept "leadership is a choice" resonate as truth?

Have you experienced leaders who are passionate about leading and who place a premium on how they lead?

Have you experienced leaders who are neglectful about leading people and who focus only on the task?

What do you understand around the Grace Hooper statement that you "manage things and lead people"?

Reflect upon whether you are more a manager of processes and things or a leader of people.

Chapter 2

Principle 2: Leadership is first a form of human relationship

Principle 1 established that leadership is a personal choice, as opposed to simply a theory or a set of principles. This means I make a conscious choice to lead; I don't take it for granted that I am doing a good job of leading just because I am in a position of leadership or authority.

Principle 2 expands on the "choice" aspect of leadership and answers the question: "Choose what?" In this chapter we establish that leadership is first a relationship. So, once I have made a deliberate and mindful choice to lead, my focus now is on my relationship with the person I am leading.

Of course, when we talk relationships, as with all relationships, the "quality" of the relationship can be measured by the positive or negative experience of both parties. In the context of leadership, by a *quality* relationship we refer specifically to the need for forming a meaningful connection which would be based on trust and mutual benefit. In this chapter we will look at the need for a relationship and in the next chapter, the quality of the connection.

I discovered this truth the hard way. Two years into leading an HR division, I attended a Stephen Covey '7 habits' course. Part of the prework was to ask my team to conduct a 360° assessment on my leadership. I was feeling confident as my team appeared to respect me and after all, I wasn't a fledgling and had led people for years. I had brought a best practice component to a floundering HR system and had received a 'Highly Effective' performance rating from the CEO himself.

The results of this assessment were enormously humbling, and fortunately were never made public. My team were polite and tactful in their feedback and whilst I received an OK assessment, I could read between the lines that all was not well. This upset me deeply and after trying to process this for a week or so, I plucked up the courage to ask my PA what she honestly thought this meant. The candid, gentle feedback she gave me was that while my team respected my knowledge, they felt that I was aloof and distant and seemed more worried about the CEO, my peers and the union than developing a relationship with my team.

Wow! While I could not argue and could see how they had come to this conclusion, I had been totally blind to their experience. I had ticked all the boxes functionally and as an executive, but I had totally failed as a leader. It was time to go back to the drawing board. When I look back, this revelation was perhaps my first step into trying to understand what it truly meant to lead and laid the foundation for developing my passion to find out as much as I could about the topic and essence of leadership.

Several years later, with a PhD under my belt, I was asked to give the keynote address at the Nelson Mandela Business School's year-end function. The topic was open – I just had to talk about leadership. I felt honoured and I was thrilled, but the more I thought about it the more the prospect stressed me out. What did I want to say about leadership, especially to a room full of academics? I was supposed to be the expert, right? As part of my research, I had completed a deep dive into leadership theory. Rather than this research settling my mind and helping me, this had left me with a distressing question: "Which theory?" While each theory had certainly provided a degree of insight, no single one of the hundreds of theories had really blown me away!

The time for the presentation was closing in on me, and I was in a panic. I am usually a confident public speaker, but on the weekend before the presentation I was still nowhere closer to answering the "which theory" question.

The challenge, I felt, was to attach myself to one theory and translate and apply what I had learned on my own leadership journey and experience where I had attained insight and self-awareness, and to present it in such a way as to enrich and inspire those in the audience!

We are privileged to live near a beautiful game reserve, the Addo Elephant Park. That Saturday, my late wife Ingrid could see that I was stressed about the presentation, so she suggested that we spend the day in the park. It was a particularly warm African summer's day and at one watering hole, over 100 elephants had gathered. Now you may know that elephants are matriarchal, so when you see large herds of elephants, you can be assured that they are predominantly female. While I watched the herd's interaction, their taking turns in the water, supervising the creche for the little ones, controlling the raucous teens and generally collaborating which each other, I began to get a sense of how their relationships work.

When the matriarch appeared, I was in awe – a huge female who was clearly the leader. She was standing a little distance away so she could watch over the goings-on of her herd. She was magnificent. She was plainly in protective mode and was very attentive.

As we watched, she began to move gently through the herd, interacting with the other females who reverently moved aside for her to pass. I was struck by a thought – this was an African version of the Gemba walk!

What do I mean by this? Interestingly, Gemba was initiated by process improvement leaders working for Toyota; it is a Japanese lean manufacturing principle, whereby the leader is fully involved in physically observing the work process on the ground level. This enables them to understand and learn about the process by asking relevant questions. This same principle seemed to be applied by the elephant matriarchal leader.

After some time, she began to move away from the watering hole, clearly deciding it was time to move on, and within a few minutes the hundred or more elephants had simply disappeared into the Eastern Cape bush. This was leadership in action, it was natural, and it was *all* about relationships!

I suppose I should have had this epiphany before, because in my own home we have five dogs. This was not my doing but I am complicit. Evidently, we had a matriarchal presence there too! I have always been amazed at how the dogs responded to me as opposed to my late wife. I would return home from work, and they would look up from the gate as if to say, "It's just him". But when my wife returned from any outing, even if she had only been away a few minutes, our dogs would go crazy with excitement. They would jump up and down as if to say, "She's back! She's back! We thought she would be out forever!"

Why the difference in the way our animals reacted to my wife and me? It comes right down to the *strength of the relationship between them*, based on the quality time she spent with them and the way she got down to their level. Since her passing I have worked hard at my relationship with our dogs and particularly our two Huskies, and the change in their reaction to me has been amazing. Even at the Husky level, connection builds trust!

It might sound bizarre to compare a human leadership relationship with that of relationships with dogs or elephants, but in line with what I explored and discussed in the preceding chapter, I am convinced that leadership goes beyond theory; it is a daily *choice*. When I intentionally made the choice to strengthen my relationship with my dogs, they began to follow and bond more with me. I am also convinced that leadership in the modern sense starts with the act of choosing to lead, and choosing to lead begins when the leader chooses to build a quality relationship with a follower, in whatever context that may exist.

> WITHOUT A QUALITY RELATIONSHIP, THERE IS NO POSSIBILITY OF
> AUTHENTIC LEADERSHIP.

Let's get technical for a moment. The word 'leadership' has two meanings:

1)   It implies either being first

     or

2)   a relationship between a leader and a follower.

Test this simple logic for yourself. Could anyone lead you meaningfully without the existence of a relationship of trust?

Most people's instinctive response to this question is a resounding NO! There simply must be some form and manifestation or expression of engagement, intent and investment in you as a person for there to be a relationship. We will drill down further and unpack this concept in the next chapter.

The exception could be people in significantly high-level positions such as politicians or executive management. I would argue, however, that while such leaders could be far removed from many of their followers, if they are good leaders they will invest heavily in building links with their followers; they will post tweets, make television appearances and continuously feature in the media. They will also lead indirectly, by leading leaders who lead others, who ultimately lead us.

During the Covid-19 pandemic, enforced social distancing put the relationship aspect of leadership into sharp focus. I have come across a wide spectrum of employee experiences, some of the most interesting of which have been in the virtual world, where in-person interactions are not possible.

Recently I coached a young woman who reflected with me on the experience of her leader's online leadership style. "She never shares her screen, and I don't really know if she is listening to me. Every time I stop speaking there is this uncomfortable moment before she picks up on the next point. I'm sure she is preoccupied and clearing her email inbox at the same time. I feel like I am just a hassle. This is not what I signed up for, but I don't know how to change her behaviour. It was so different when we were in the office together."

I'm sure you would agree that if leadership is first a relationship, then in this disconnected world, we leaders really are compelled to try harder. We need to be mindful of our people and the quality of our communication experience.

People in leadership positions who lose sight of the importance of connecting are bound to experience loss of much of the support they might have built up in the past. It is often said that "people don't leave companies, they leave managers". Could this be a reason why so many employees changed companies during the pandemic? In the USA, this is now termed "The Great Resignation" – statistics show that 3% of their entire workforce quit their jobs in September 2021.

Clearly, the Covid pandemic has highlighted to us how important it is for leaders to maintain engaged relationships with their followers.

I have met team members who have not spoken to their leaders for lengthy periods, the exception being perhaps the monthly departmental meeting. Some have had a token monthly engagement with their leader, who appears in the form of a Microsoft Team's dot, usually demanding report back and coming across as unapproachable. I met a new team member who after four months still had no idea of what his leader or team members look like. These examples demonstrate how easily leaders can totally neglect the foundational relationship component of their responsibilities.

Humans are social beings and while we each have our functional responsibilities, it is in our relationships with others where we can be made to feel valued and nurtured.

In my coaching sessions during this period, I have also encountered many examples of leaders taking the time to check in with their team members, stepping in when they encounter difficulties and tragedies, and really making the effort to make a difference. This is in stark contrast to many examples where leaders in the online virtual world transformed into white spots in team meetings, never sharing their screens or making human connections.

With the **choice** to lead comes the second principle – the obligation to **build meaningful relationships** with team members, as well as facilitate the connections between them.

IF YOU CHOOSE TO LEAD, THEN IT MUST FOLLOW THAT YOU CHOOSE TO BUILD TRUST-BASED RELATIONSHIPS.

So, what do these leadership relationships look like? In the next few chapters, we will look at the quality of these relationships in practice, having accepted that leadership is not just a theory but a state of mind!

Leadership is a choice

Reflection Exercise

Principle 2: Leadership is first a relationship!

Do you agree with this idea? Illustrate.

Have you experienced great leaders in your life who were not invested in their relationship with you and who you felt did not care about you?

Reflect on the leader who had the most profound positive impact on your life. To what extent was this leader invested in your mutual relationship?

Reflect upon how you could use this principle in practice.

| |
| |
| |
| |

Chapter 3

Principle 3: Relationships are about connection and trust

At this juncture we have established that leadership is a choice or a calling, as opposed to a theory (Principle 1). In the second chapter we examined the idea that our leadership choice starts with establishing a relationship with the people we are called to lead. Without this key relationship with those entrusted to our leadership, we are unable to lead (Principle 2).

Building upon these ideas, this chapter will look deeper into the core and nature of these relationships and how the *quality* of relationships is measured by the level of trust we have in the person we are in a relationship with. This magic ingredient, trust, emerges (or not) because of our experience of the other person. We call this **connection**.

I experienced this in a very entertaining way just prior to Covid-19 when I took a flight from Bloemfontein to Johannesburg. Because Bloemfontein is the legislative capital of South Africa, when you take the 45 min flight to Johannesburg you usually share the plane with lawyers and advocates. On this day there were several distinctly "legal eagle" types on the flight. One guy particularly caught my attention. Perhaps it was his striking powder blue suit, power haircut and designer glasses, or perhaps it was the way he strutted up and down in front of the other passengers, pulling along his "legal" type briefcase and talking animatedly on his mobile phone. Whatever it was, I found that I immediately took a dislike to his arrogant persona. A lady opposite me noticed my reaction and rolled her eyes in subtle agreement with me.

When our flight was called, the guy in the blue suit played the priority boarding card and went and stood in the front of the 20 or so passengers. He continued talking on the phone while he fumbled around for his ticket which he had not thought of keeping on hand. We all waited patiently. He then walked slowly to the plane, still on the phone, oblivious of the rest of the passengers. We all lined up after him, politely following at an irritating snail's pace behind him. When he boarded the plane, we all waited patiently again while he struggled to get the big black briefcase into the overhead stowage, all the while continuing his loud telephone conversation. Finally, he sat down and the rest of us boarded. Wouldn't you know, I ended up in the seat behind him and less than five minutes after take-off he dropped his seat right back into my lap. He was totally oblivious of me or any discomfort he may be causing a fellow passenger on this small plane and brief flight.

As soon as we landed Blue Suit jumped up and grabbed his briefcase from the overhead locker and began pushing forward. The woman from the departures area who had noticed my irritation and rolled her eyes at me had been seated a few rows ahead of us and as Blue Suit tried to push past her, she turned around and loudly protested, "You! Who do you think you are? You – You can wait your turn!"

All the passengers went quiet for a moment, and then someone at the back of the plane began a slow clap; soon many passengers were doing the same.

I realised in that moment that based on Blue Suit's attitude – his *connection* – everyone on the plane had come to the same conclusion... this guy is an "A-hole". We had all experienced Blue Suit's indirect connection and had subconsciously come to dislike and distrust him. Would you follow him if he was your leader?

> AS SOCIAL BEINGS, HUMANS MAKE SUBCONSCIOUS ASSESSMENTS ABOUT ONE OTHER BASED UPON OUR CONNECTION. THESE ASSESSMENTS EITHER AMOUNT TO TRUST, OR DISTRUST.

I use the term *connection* because, as opposed to communication or engagement, I intend to cover the full ambit of the human experience one person may have of another.

Let me explain. We have five identifiable senses: sight, smell, touch, taste and hearing. We also possess an intuitive sense, which may manifest when we combine input from all our senses into an instinctual or 'feeling' interpretation of what our senses have absorbed. This intuition is based, and thus formed, on the *words* the other person uses, their *actions* and *behaviour*, their *body language*, their *personal expressions*, their *scent* and even their outward appearance – the way they *dress*. In a nutshell, intuition seeks out every clue that our five senses can identify. The sum of all the interactions which someone may experience from another, we call *connection*.

There is a great deal of research about connection, which either facilitates or hinders trust. Think about this universal principle for a moment – with every action there is an equal and opposite reaction. When a connection occurs based on a lived experience with another person, we respond, and this response is at a subliminal level. Based on *how* I experience you, I react psychologically. I will either be inclined to like you and develop a level of trust in you, or I will respond with dislike and ultimately distrust.

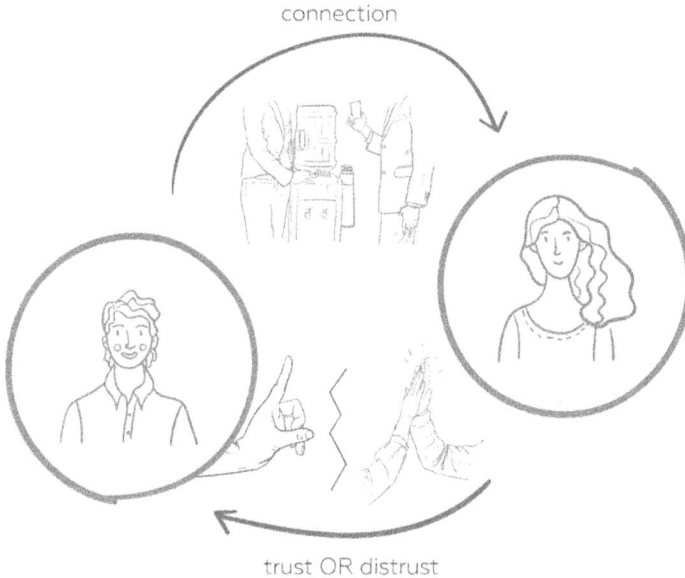

This simple diagram describes relationships at their most basic level. I connect with you and over time you develop a dominant impression of me. Either you like/trust me or you dislike/distrust me.

Let's talk about trust for a moment.

How important is trust to you? Do you work better, think more clearly, or find more pleasure in life when you are trusted? Absolutely! When you trust the people with whom you are working do you feel and are you more empowered? No question! So, what is this abstract called 'trust'? There are numerous definitions and studies on trust. Trust is increasingly recognised as the key component within healthy and meaningful human relationships, particularly relationships in the workplace where there is some level of production or output involved.

Let's flesh out what trust is and how it is established. Some time ago I needed to purchase a used car for my son. The first dealer I went to kept on saying to me, "You can trust me! I have been in this business for 30 years, trust me when I say...". Strangely and counterproductively, the more he insisted that I should trust him, the less I did. His 'hard sell' attitude really put me off. I then went to a used car dealer who a friend recommended, and the experience was completely different. Instead of trying to hard sell me what he had in his lot, he carefully listened to my needs and then, when he did not have the ideal vehicle for me at his dealership, he negotiated on my behalf with a competitor to ensure I got the ideal purchase!

On reflection it is clear to me that you cannot tell or persuade someone to trust you, much less demand it, simply because you hold a position, title or qualification. It isn't what you say, it's what you do! Proverbially, actions speak louder than words, and this cannot be underestimated. Real and genuine trust is the product of our authentic interactions and integrity in connections.

Whilst much has been written on this subject, I find the research by Zenger Folkman[2] most useful. They examined the 360° assessments of some 87,000 leaders and identified a cluster of three components that they believed were most often the foundation for trust: **positive relationships,** good judgement/expertise and consistency.

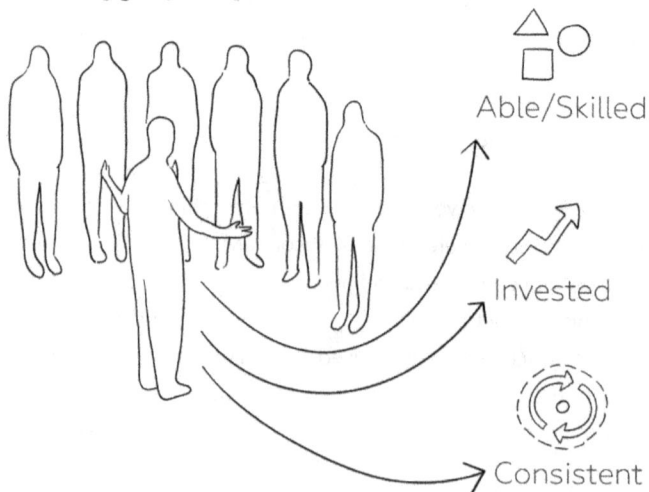

I trust a leader who is...

Able/Skilled

Invested

Consistent

Let's examine these elements and how the way in which we connect with each other builds each component:

> **Positive relationships**: *In positive relationships there exists an authentic sense that the other person is genuinely invested in our mutual relationship.*

> I have, on several occasions, reported to or worked with peers who are totally self-driven and self-absorbed. Was I able to work with such people? Yes, I was, but that was pretty much because I was paid to do so. Would I have preferred to work with someone whom I trusted to have my best interests at heart? Absolutely!

> We quickly and instinctively know if someone is invested in us. Do they show interest in us when they make small talk? Do they listen? Does my opinion count for anything? Unless we are particularly naive, we also get a distinct sense when someone is driven by self-interest.

> Good judgement/expertise: *The tangible sense that the other person is able/competent and knows what they are doing and are honest and transparent when they do not.*

For a few years I reported to the nicest expat MD, David. He established warm relationships with people and was genuinely concerned about our well-being. He would spend hours chatting to us and getting to know us at a personal level. He would very often give unsolicited gifts such as excess packs of venison after he had been on a hunting trip. At a personal level I considered him to be a close friend. He had replaced a self-centred tyrant, and so initially I was thrilled to be working with this friendly person.

Sadly however, as time went on, we began to realise that David was making poor, impetuous decisions and his judgement was not mature enough for an organisation of this size and scale. He would make purchases the company could not afford and go on trips which were of no value at all. He would miss key meetings and his numbers were very suspect. Working with him was a nightmare on this level and while I genuinely liked him, I felt I could not trust his judgement. I made sure my work contributions were distinct from his for the sake of clarity. To survive, the production manager and I essentially ran the organisation without him being aware of it, managing head office relationships and operations. The takeout from this is that while at a personal level, ability and competence may not be key for a trusting relationship, in the workplace it's different. When another person's actions and decisions are based on bad judgement and have a negative impact on yourself and the company, no matter how "nice" they are, their ability and competence or lack thereof contributes to either engendering trust or precluding it.

Consistency: *The other person is stable and reliable and their attitude does not fluctuate on a whim.*

In Afrikaans we have a saying: "Sy aand en oggend praatjies stem nie ooreen nie." Translated directly – what he says in the evening is incongruent with what he says in the morning. I am sure that, like me, you have had the experience where someone who treated you as if you were a close friend inexplicably shifted allegiance when a more important or attractive person came on the scene. This confuses and derails.

Consistent leaders are consistent in ethics, in standards, in integrity. They are clear about what they want and where they are going, and this consistency gives us comfort. We are able to function with confidence because we always know where we stand, because it is clear where the leader stands on all key issues.

Think about it for a minute. How would I know if you are trustworthy? In other words, whether you are invested in our relationship and whether you are able and consistent? I would have to make a judgement based upon my real lived experience of you. How you talk to me, what you do and how you behave when you are under pressure are some factors that would indicate whether you are consistent and reliable or not. In other words, it is what I experience when I connect with you.

Time, of course, plays a role in how things pan out. We know that first impressions are real. Over time however, these initial impressions can either be reinforced or adjusted, depending on our experience of a person over time.

This dynamic is constantly at play everywhere people engage one another; from the chance encounter in a shopping centre, at a pub or in a gym, or in the case of kids in a play area, to a place of worship and of course, the workplace.

I recently moved to a small coastal village, Bushman's River Mouth, on the east coast of South Africa. As a newcomer to the area, I was invited to a braai (South African barbeque). My date and I met an entire group of new people and on the way home we shared our dominant impressions of the people we had been introduced to. Our post-mortem discussion may have sounded something like this: "Don't you think Xolile has an awesome sense of humour?" "I really enjoyed Sarah and James, and think they could be great friends." "I found Johnny rather stuck-up and hard to relate to, I don't think he is my type."

However, subsequent connections with Johnny have shown things in a different light. I met him in the supermarket a week later and this encounter altered my experience and initial impression of him. He is clearly more comfortable in a one-on-one context, and we chatted for a while and agreed to go fishing together. My dominant initial impression of "stuck-up" significantly changed to, "Actually, Johnny is a sincere chap".

Johnny subsequently confided in me that he is shy in larger groups and felt very out of place at our first encounter. He was aware that he had come over badly and had resolved to intentionally choose to connect differently. That choice resulted in his projecting warmth and openness.

The consequence of getting to know Johnny and his social vulnerability is endearing. He is now someone whom I really trust, and we have shared some deep personal experiences in our conversations. Johnny's awareness of how he comes over and how he then chose to connect was an important factor in my changing my opinion of him.

We all know the adage about judging a book by its cover, so it is important that we be mindful to take some time to allow for adjustments in our perspective, connection and trust on a deeper level. My new friend made a choice in connecting despite his introversion, which contributed to a trusting, two-way relationship. This is the kind of dynamic relationship of trust we strive for as leaders.

The notion of leaders taking responsibility for *how* they connect with people is discussed in the next chapter.

Reflection Exercise

Principle 3: Relationships are about connection and trust

Make a list of people you know; some you have met recently and some you have known for a while. Reflect on your dominant impression of them. Why do you feel this way and what do you base this opinion on?

Does this concept resonate as truth: "I connect with you and based on your experience you respond with trust or distrust." Explain.

Test what is your lived experience when it comes to trusting people.

Reflect on these questions: What dominant impression do I leave with the people I meet:

- for the first time; and

- as time passes?

Reflect upon how you could use this awareness could help you in practice.

Chapter 4

Principle 4: Within a leadership relationship the leader is responsible for the relationship

In the previous chapter we looked at relationships in general and how our trust or distrust in the other person emerges over time, based on how we experience them. When I present this in class, I ask the question, "Is there a difference between a relationship between a leader and his/her team member and a relationship between peers?" Do the same two elements of connection and trust apply? In other words, I connect with you and over time you learn to trust or distrust me, and vice versa.

In my class this question always opens up a debate. Some strongly claim that there should be no difference between a leadership relationship and a relationship with peers. Others think it's a trick question. In this chapter we will examine the subtle difference, and up front I want to caution that this difference is perhaps the most important leadership insight.

Let's consider the most basic leadership role – that of parent and child. Can the child initiate the relationship if the parent does not create the opportunity for connection? I very much doubt that, and the many children of absent fathers in our country would testify to this. The same dynamic exists in the workplace. It can be extremely difficult for a subordinate to initiate connection with a superior, but it's much simpler and seems more natural for the superior to do so.

In the Covid-19 social distance experience, would it be easy for the team member to call their leader up and ask how they were doing? One can imagine that this might be awkward and the gesture may possibly appear forward. The other way around, where the leader checks in on a team member, is most likely to feel more natural. If the leader takes the initiative to make such a call, it would probably be perceived as caring and empathetic.

When you and I sign up for a leadership position and accept the pay slip, we accept accountability at the same time. I want to stress that this accountability is not just for the output of the role. This is not simply about getting the job or assignment done; I am referring to a different aspect of responsibility, and that is the actual relationship between us as a leader and our subordinates.

Let's examine the logic. If leadership is a choice (Principle 1) and it is also a relationship (Principle 2), and relationships are foundationally built on the trust connection (Principle 3), then logically it follows that if I am the appointed leader, then I must accept accountability for the relationship first and foremost. The leader, not the follower, is compelled and obligated to be responsible for the quality of the relationship, not the other way around.

To be effective in the modern business world a leader needs to be trusted, and this trust can only emerge as a result of our choice to connect with our followers. As we discussed above, it is far easier for us as a leader to initiate the relationship than for a follower to do so. Frankly, I don't believe that it can ever really work the other way around.

Over and above this practical one-sidedness, we can deduce that the distinct difference in roles between team member and leader is accountability. So, in essence, there is a primary responsibility for the relationship which rests squarely on our shoulders as leaders. It is we who must take the initiative to nurture the relationship.

WHEN AN EMPLOYEE IS PROMOTED INTO A LEADERSHIP POSITION, THE NEW MANAGER ACCEPTS THE NEW PAYSLIP WITH THE NEW TITLE. ALONG WITH THAT TITLE THERE IS AN IMPLIED RESPONSIBILITY TO LEAD A TEAM OF PEOPLE.

This is illustrated as follows.

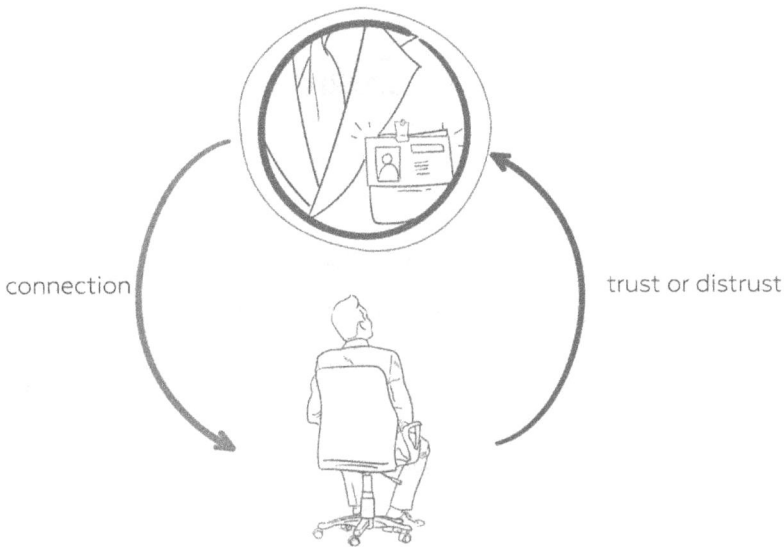

connection   trust or distrust

While this diagram depicts the same elements as the previous principle in Chapter 3, here 'connection and trust' is assigned to the leader and not the subordinate to bear this responsibility. The overarching goal is that our subordinates respond to us with trust.

"All good and well", you may say, "but what about the other way round, what about my trust in the subordinate?" While relevant, this is not a chicken and egg quandary. When we provide our subordinate with a positive lived experience that makes him/her *want* to follow our direction, we have succeeded in building trust. And when that happens, we will have no reason to distrust our team member as they commit to following our lead.

We, the leader, not the subordinate, have signed up for and accepted a specific responsibility. It says so on our payslip. Our title – manager, supervisor, director, headmaster, whatever – implies that we have accepted responsibility for a leadership relationship. **When as leaders we accept this responsibility, it colours everything we do.**

Reflection Exercise

Principle 4: In a leadership relationship the leader is responsible for the relationship

Does it resonate as truth that the leader and not the subordinate is responsible for the quality of the relationship? Explain.

Is this true in your lived experience?

Reflect upon how you could use this idea in practice.

Chapter 5

Principle 5: Leaders build trust through switching off auto pilot and deliberately connecting

Recently I was contacted by a young woman whom we shall call Di. She had just been promoted to a position of leadership and was desperate. "I'm just not good at this leadership stuff", she explained. "I know how to do my job, but this leadership relationship business is next level." I think this is the common experience of most people who take up their first formal leadership position.

I took Di through the logic pertaining to the four principles we have established thus far. "That's great", she responded, "it all makes sense and I'm in, but ok, so what now?"

For the new leader, and in fact all leaders, the practical aspect of this can be a real challenge.

Our organisations tend to focus on short-term results and measurements – shareholders' returns, sales targets, profitability, volumes, quality measurements and so on. As we discussed in Chapter 1, we *manage processes and systems* and we *lead people*. If you work in a corporate environment, it is likely that your life is, to a large extent, driven by endless KPIs and project deadlines. As leaders this keeps us occupied and focused. The management aspect is constantly on the agenda, it drives our diaries, and we need to be effective or we quickly lose credibility. Make no mistake, in any position of leadership in a competitive environment, if we are not effective managers we will battle to survive.

The other side of the coin is the leadership relationship. This dimension could ultimately emerge as being more important and carry even more weight than the daily management stuff. However, while this vital element distinguishes leaders from management administrators, and as we discuss later will establish a sustainable competitive advantage, this side is of the coin is seldom measured.

Let's reflect for a moment. The first five principles build the argument for a personal leadership strategy, which is based on the relationship between the leader and their subordinate:

To recap, steps 1 to 5 are:

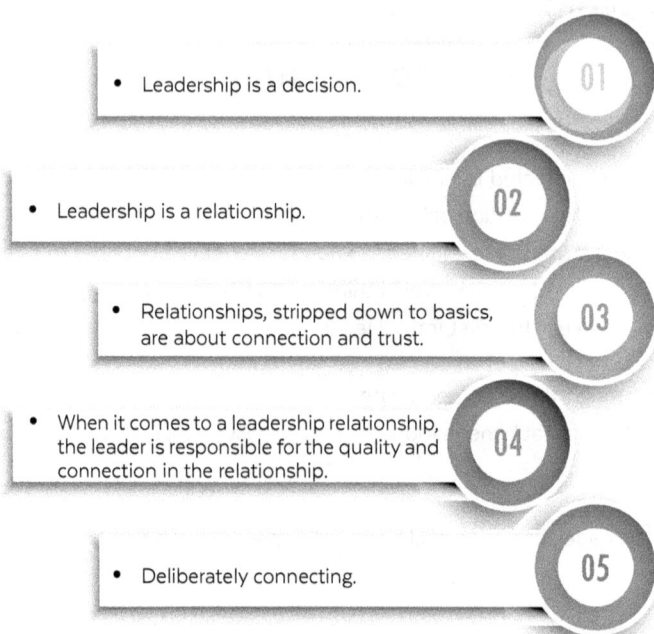

- Leadership is a decision.

  01

- Leadership is a relationship.

  02

- Relationships, stripped down to basics, are about connection and trust.

  03

- When it comes to a leadership relationship, the leader is responsible for the quality and connection in the relationship.

  04

- Deliberately connecting.

  05

So, the question is, how does this work in practice? How do I, as a leader, build on the first four steps *and truly connect* with team members? This is a key question, and the answer will be unique to each of us. Some leaders seem to successfully connect and build relationships while others struggle to do so. Why is that the case? What can be done to solve this dilemma?

While the practical application of leadership connection will be unique to each of us, I believe that there is a key underpinning criterion which will be the difference between successful leadership and having good intentions but experiencing a constant struggle. Let's unpack this further.

WHY DO WE CONNECT EASILY WITH CERTAIN PEOPLE AND NOT WITH OTHERS?

Reflect on this – why do you find it easy to connect with some people and not with others?

I have explored this question extensively and a few common themes have emerged.

- **Personality**: some people are just nice and easy to get on with. They could be people whose personalities and values are much like ours, or they are just pleasant to be around and are largely easy to connect with.

- **Background**: we seem to connect more easily with people we have grown up with, who attended the same schools or universities, who have worked in the same company, or who attend the same spiritual, political or sports institutions. As a young man I was privileged to spend some time in Germany on an internship. I made great friends with a Nigerian fellow student; our only common connection point was that we were both from Africa.

- **Interests**: we find it easy to connect with people who share our interests. Sport, music, hobbies, clubs and so forth are all common points of interest which make connection easier. I am amazed, for instance, at how women develop lifelong relationships formed during shared antenatal classes.

- **Experiences**: when we have gone through difficult experiences together, we seem to be able to move beyond the initial barriers more easily to meaningful connection. It has been my experience that there is nothing like a nightmare flight with extreme turbulence to turn a plane full of strangers into a tightly bonded group of survivors.

While these natural connections are personally positive human experiences, they are not always guaranteed to organically emerge.

So where does leadership come in on this theme?

There will always be certain people we just don't relate to so easily. Let's be honest, it is perfectly normal for us to connect more easily with some people than with others. So, in a group of 10 people it is probable that you could rank them in order of those who you find you are strongly connected to, those you have a natural relationship with, and still others with whom you have no connection at all.

This is perhaps okay if you are in a situation where relationships are not foundational to its effectiveness and success. However, when it comes to leadership, we have already determined that leadership is first and foremost about relationships, and that the quality of those relationship is up to the leader.

As it is in life outside of work, it stands to reason that we as leaders will find some in our team easier to connect with than others. This is why it is necessary to deliberately and mindfully make connection part of our leadership persona.

So, is it okay that we connect with some and not with others? It most definitely isn't! Reflect on the following consequences if we followed that line of reasoning.

- Subordinate disengagement

  If you have ever been part of the "out" group in any social structure, you will know that being less connected to your leader than others on the team is very uncomfortable; it can be damaging to your confidence, lonely and even annoying. It is likely that you will be less engaged and give less of yourself to the team.

  According to a Gallup employee engagement survey, up to 70% of people in our organisations are disengaged. This is a staggering statistic and a massive challenge. The question is, would a connected leadership relationship make a difference? I believe this is a no-brainer.

- Negative subgroup formation

  When people experience that they are not part of the "in crowd", it is likely that they gravitate towards others who feel the same lack of connection to the leader. This is how negative 'subgroups' develop in a team. This may result in a 'team cancer' which can negate and contaminate all the good the leader is trying to accomplish.

  It stands to reason that when an "in group" and an "out group" emerge within a team its functionality is negatively affected.

  During my many years in HR this was probably one of the most common causes of team issues and conflict. This is most often the problem that emerges when facilitating emergency team building interventions. Such a fallout is very difficult to reverse because when this dynamic is at play, trust in the leader may be fragile. All too often, he or she will very likely suffer reputationally.

A cautionary tale from personal experience

You may be thinking that you are a great 'people person', you find developing relationships easy, and that this team relationship dysfunction is unlikely to happen to you. Don't be too sure. Sadly, in my own experience, my over-confidence in this area meant that I took my ability to connect for granted, and consequently I failed spectacularly.

Some years ago, I was headhunted to lead the HR function of a large manufacturing organisation. Before I had to any degree built relationships with my new team of HR experts, I was assigned to lead a component of a massive and critical tender process. For three months I was working 18+ hours days on this exciting challenge. While running the background script that I knew I needed to build relationships with my team, I was physically run off my feet. It was also a very confidential process, so I was not able to share anything of what I was doing with any of the HR team members.

I was, however, confident that they would understand, and so I felt that the sooner this process resolved itself the sooner I would get back to having an impact on the team. Boy, was I ever wrong! The three month absence did more damage than I could ever have imagined. I quickly discovered that the authentic personality I believed I had cultivated, and which had so easily built relationships in the past, was perceived to be false and my absent leadership was considered a serious breach of trust. This experience was a real learning curve for me and has grounded and cemented my conviction that relying on one's natural ability to connect and build a trusted leadership relationship is fatally flawed.

So far in this chapter I have maintained that leadership is based on a relationship and that the ability to connect with someone is fundamental to establishing a relationship with that person. I also touched on how we have reasons for easily connecting with some people and difficulty in connecting with others, and that in line with the responsibility to lead, random connection is not an option if it excludes some team members. I have also discussed some of the common problems that arise when leaders connect selectively with some subordinates and not with others, and illustrated this from my own personal experience.

If we accept principles 1 to 4 to any degree, then it is clear that to lead effectively and successfully we need to build relationships with **all** our team members, not just those with whom we have a natural connection.

So, what is the solution? If 'natural connection' can prove to be a slippery slope in a leadership context, what is the alternative? The answer is quite simple – that we, the leader, truly commit to deliberate, conscious connection. It starts with a *decision* to connect and continues with a *process* of setting up disciplined actions which continue to build connection with each and every team member. Deliberate connection means that we switch off the auto pilot of everyday management and deliberately/consciously connect relationally with every subordinate. The below diagram illustrates this concept.

ONLY IF WE DELIBERATELY AND CONSCIOUSLY CONNECT CAN WE BE SURE OF BUILDING PRODUCTIVE TRUST-BASED RELATIONSHIPS WITH TEAM MEMBERS.

natural
connection
- personality
- background
- experience

switch off autopilot!

How does this work in practice?

There are literally thousands of little things, gestures and activities that we could implement and apply. The challenge is that this is, and should be, deliberate and mindful. We need to create and follow a consistent, almost habitual, routine of connecting with each subordinate. In just about everything we engage in with our team there is a choice to execute the activity with a mindset of 'management' or just getting the job done, or to adopt a 'leadership' mindset. The management mindset says, "let me connect with the task" while the leadership mindset says, "let me connect with the person".

If we adopt a leadership mindset, then every time we engage an employee we exercise leadership in a subtle way. This essentially means that we need to take care to listen, show interest, make eye contact and be conscious of how we assert ourselves. The tone of our emails, how we lead meetings and even how we dress has an impact.

Here are some examples of deliberate acts of connection by leaders that I have seen impact positively on people, but you need to establish your own tools:

- During the Covid-19 lockdown, the most successful leaders I know of established brief daily virtual check-ins with their teams.
- Walking the floor of the factory daily and engage with people about their lives.
- Remembering birthdays, secretary day, personal events, etc.
- Attending funerals.
- Arranging team building and social activities.
- Departmental meetings.
- Short stand up meetings.
- One-on-one discussions about future development.
- Making eye contact when greeting everyone in the morning.
- Knowing every name of the personnel in a big department.
- Following up on events, weddings, people in hospital, pregnancies, etc.
- A treat out of your own pocket after hard work.
- Writing a heartfelt thank-you note.
- Including a personal letter of thanks with salary increases.
- An extra special effort with retirements or resignations.
- Fetching food from the canteen to save people spending their lunch break waiting in line.
- Publicly using Facebook or Instagram to connect and show a human face.
- Inviting team members to your home for a meal.

This list is by no means exhaustive and as you contemplate the individuals in your team, it would be good to generate your own ideas to implement. These simple acts of connection are more significant and impactful than you may realise. Perhaps the most stunning example I experienced of this type of deliberate connection concerned a colleague of mine who was head of a manufacturing unit. He was responsible for about 350 employees who were mostly 50+, relatively poor women who had been with the company for many years. He initiated the practice of having a one-on-one audience with each employee on their birthday, and set up a system to ensure that this never fell through the cracks. He would spend around 45 minutes talking to the employee about their personal life, their children and their spouses. He engaged them on matters such as how long they had been at the company, where they lived, their hobbies and interests, the stuff of life. At the end of the session, he would reach into the box he kept under the table and give the employee a large slab of chocolate. Unbeknown to him the employee would return to the line proudly waving the gift of chocolate for everyone to see.

When this manager left the company, the entire workforce did something I had never seen before. They stood at the window of the factory and beat rhythmically with their hands in a gesture of respect and goodwill. The tangible sense was that these workers would have walked through fire for the company and their leader.

How you develop connection with your team needs to reflect yourself, and should be an authentic action rather than something that feels contrived. But authenticity does not mean that only the spontaneous counts. If you are committed to and intend to strengthen your leadership relationships, then any action you will take will be authentic.

> WHEN DELIBERATELY CONNECTING, MOST OFTEN SIMPLE, CONSISTENT, DISCIPLINED HABITS ACHIEVE GREATER RESULTS THAN GRAND GESTURES.

In summary, it is fair to say that connection is human, and we all naturally connect to certain people in our world based on different factors such as personality, backgrounds, interests and experiences. Natural connection means, however, that we connect with some people and not others. While that's okay in our private lives, it's not if we are responsible for building a team. The solution is to practice deliberate acts of connection and do this consistently!

Reflection Exercise

Principle 5: Leaders build trust through switching off auto pilot and deliberately connecting

How well do you connect with team members? Illustrate.

Do you connect with all team members equally? Explain briefly.

Are you open to deliberately building connection with all team members? Why?

Reflect upon how you could use this idea in practice. Brainstorm 10 deliberate connecting actions you can practice regularly with your team.

1.	
2.	
3.	
4.	
5.	
6.	
7.	
8.	
9.	
10.	

Chapter 6

Principle 6: Leadership moments amplify the connection/trust experience

Having come as far as principle 6, it is possible that you may have concluded that this deliberate connection will work as long as everything is smooth sailing. However, as we know, that is not the real world and life is not always a well-oiled machine. So what options are open to us when the inevitable crises and challenges come along? What do we need to do when the relationship wheels come off, or when a team member needs to be disciplined, or worse, retrenched? How will we leaders respond when someone passes away or employees' relationships collapse? When life happens and things are challenging, simple connections will not automatically deliver a solution.

I want to emphasise here that leadership, and especially *relationship-focused leadership*, will continuously be stressed, challenged and put under the spotlight.

WE CALL THESE MOMENTS "LEADERSHIP MOMENTS"

Leadership moments are those instances when *what* we as leaders do in a specific moment of challenge has a considerable impact upon the trust that has been emerging with our followers. What we do in such circumstances will count significantly.

Why are leadership moments so important?

We trust leaders who are able, and our ability as a leader is significantly exposed when we face leadership moments. Even when we have, as discussed in the previous chapter, been deliberate in building trust-based relationships, failure to respond appropriately when faced with a leadership moment can significantly damage that trust. When facing leadership moments, our good judgement is crucial! While it can be said that we may likely become more adept and practiced at handling leadership moments, with time there is always a risk that we miscalculate our response in the heat of the moment.

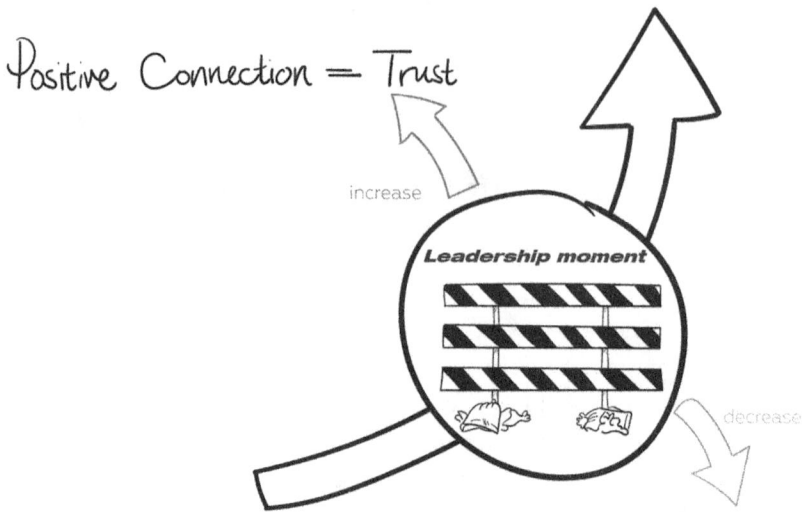

Positive Connection = Trust

This illustration depicts the certainty that while we are building positive relationships, we will encounter "roadblocks" to leadership moments. How we respond and act in such moments will either increase or reduce the trust our followers put in us.

Reflect for a moment. Can you remember a time when your leader specifically acted in a way that made you question the trust you had in him/her? I can recount many such moments, but I can also recall positive moments when my trust in a leader was enhanced as a result of the leader's finesse and sensitivity in handling a difficult situation, even when the result was not in my personal favour.

I can clearly remember the grief I felt after we had made a board decision that meant retrenchments were inevitable. While I know that corporates are obligated to do whatever possible to avoid going this route, I was resigned to the fact that in this matter we had no alternative. I was the Human Resource Director. This was my job and it fell on me to execute this painful decision. This was honestly the most awful situation I had experienced in my work life so far. I truly felt heartbroken for these people. I had worked so hard to build something special in our company and now employees were going to lose their source of income.

This was the last thing I wanted to do. If I could have run away, I would have. I can remember sending up a heartfelt prayer: "Please take this cup from me." In my mind, I had clear insight: "You, Charles, are equipped to do this because your intent is to manage the situation and the people affected, with empathy."

This was a leadership moment; a moment when my leadership was in the spotlight. My leadership would be defined by how I responded and therefore how I would be perceived as a leader going forward by our workforce.

While I could never feel proud of such an assignment, I do know that the inevitable outcome of the process, whilst truly unfortunate, was recognised by everyone involved, as the only course to follow.

This was one of the major leadership moments in my life.

As illustrated above, a leadership moment is any moment which occurs during your term as a leader when *how* you manage the moment will significantly increase, or alternatively damage, the trust your team members have in you.

As leaders these moments will manifest often, and although they take on a multitude of different forms, they have a few things in common.

- A leadership moment is an event.

- A leadership moment requires the leader to decide what impacts upon a subordinate or subordinates.

- A leadership moment has the potential to be resolved either well or badly.

- While we may have an instinctive response to leadership moments, they are generally better managed when careful thought and planning are invested into them.

Whereas some of these leadership moments are substantial and significant, there are other moments which are more commonplace. Either way, when we take on a leadership role, we sign up on to take responsibility for these leadership moments – big or small – and their impact on people. We can learn to dread this element of leadership or embrace it. How we embrace and deal with leadership moments is what defines us leaders.

Here are some examples of common leadership moments.

- Performance review discussions
- A bereavement
- Conflict among staff members

- A key resignation
- Chairing an important meeting
- Quality issues
- A new employee onboarding
- A disciplinary hearing
- An employee experiencing personal stress
- Any organisational change
- A new process
- Change of management
- An accident
- A change of office layout
- The annual year end function
- A daily stand-up meeting

The list is endless...

How do I address a 'leadership moment'?

Remember that during leadership moments, we are looking to build or at least sustain the trust our team members have in us. Using the three key elements of trust discussed in Chapter 2, *Able, Invested and Consistent*, we need to ensure the following:

1. We are displaying some level of finesse or wisdom because people trust leaders who are able to handle the difficult moments.

2. We need to display to our team members that we are invested in their best interests. We trust people who we believe have our best interests at heart. (While this may not always be absolutely possible as organisational dynamics do sometime override individual interests, we need to show that we are aware of the individual interests and have carefully weighed the choices we make.)

3. We need to display that we are consistent with our ethics and even-handed in our dealings with different team members. We also need to display that we are consistent in the standards we set and expect.

Having brainstormed leadership moments with a number of leaders, with the objective of finding good principles and ways of enhancing trust while dealing with difficult moments, I have identified a few key principles.

'Leadership moment' principles

What makes real leaders stand out is their passion to use every leadership moment as an opportunity to build connection and trust.

1. **Never walk past**

While avoiding conflict and confrontation or challenging situations is a common human response, every time we do that, our leadership credibility is compromised. So, the first principle of leadership moments is never to walk past that opportunity.

This implies that we do not rush headlong into a situation without careful forethought, but rather that we recognise the leadership moment before us, accept it, and be mindful that our choice of action will either enhance or compromise our leadership relationship.

2. **Focus on the issue**

The secret to any ball skill is keeping our eye on the ball. The same principle applies to leadership moments – focus on the issue. But what does this mean?

If a subordinate is grieving, what is the issue? The issue in this context is not the symptom, i.e., the employee is distracted at work. The issue that needs addressing is that this person you as a leader are responsible for is suffering, and as such you should be impelled to offer appropriate compassion and empathy for the bereaved.

If a subordinate is under-performing, the issue is not *what* they are failing at but *why* this is the case. So instead of merely seeing the symptom, you should be examining the cause, or root, of the problem.

3. **Pass the ball, don't play it**

This principle is about managing our reaction to a leadership moment.

There are many instances where it may be justifiable to be reactive in a leadership moment, but remember, our reaction will impact not only on the subordinates directly involved, but on every other person who observes our behaviour and reaction.

When we are impulsively reactive to a leadership moment, and especially when our reaction has a knee-jerk, emotional element to it, it is likely that the focus, in the moment, shifts to the leader and not the situation and the relationship.

We call this "playing the ball".

When we as leaders become emotionally engaged or disrespectful while managing a leadership moment, a loss of trust in us as a leader will not be confined only to those directly involved in the situation, but will impact on all the parties observing from a distance.

It is therefore a good idea to avoid dressing down an employee in public, as an audience will in many cases impact upon how the employee responds.

I propose two variations of approach for the leader to employ to address issues of concern and force accountability. These approaches are highly preferable to aggressive or high-handed reactions, which often lead to defensive counter-reactions.

Approach 1: Use questions rather than accusations

I like the idea of using questions to shift accountability to the follower rather than outright attacking the person:

Playing the man		Playing the ball
That presentation was a total disgrace	or	Did you feel that was your best presentation?
How many times must I tell you to go and study?	or	Do you have an exam tomorrow?
Your performance has been terrible this quarter	or	Is there a reason why you are off this month's targets?

The beauty of this approach is that the person is held accountable. When your team member feels attacked, whatever the reason, there is a real danger that you, the leader, will end up looking like an unreasonable person or worse, a bully, and the person may disengage and feel resentful towards you.

Approach 2: Use "I" statements as opposed to "You" statements

I first encountered "I" statements when I was confronted by a business partner who really felt I had let him down, but he did so without destroying the relationship. We had worked alongside each other for some time, and we had reached the stage that it made business sense to combine our two businesses. On the day that we were to sign a partnership agreement, I backed out. I decided it was just not what I really wanted. He was furious, but confronted me in such a way that I was honestly hard-pressed to take offence.

He said, *"Charles, it is my perception that you are misusing our relationship. It is my perception"*, he continued, *"that you take more than you give, and it is further my perception that you have misled me..."*.

He then rounded this off with a spectacular: *"I would like you to think about my perceptions and call me tomorrow with your response."*

What he had done was to express his anger and frustration, but he had not wrecked our relationship in doing so.

Read the same confrontation but drop the "I" statement ('my perception') and the entire engagement feels completely different.

"Charles, you are misusing our relationship, you take more than you give, and you have misled me..."

How do you rebuild a relationship from here?

When you are in a position of leadership and you feel angry and that you really need to sound off and address an employee's actions or attitude, you run the risk of sounding arrogant, tyrannical or unreasonable. "You" statements are normally met with some form of defensive response and seldom really make a subordinate self-reflect or accept accountability. However, "I" statements are different. "I" statements cannot be met with a defensive response. Instead, they compel the other party to explain him or herself, or at least accept some level of accountability. "You" statements make the problem bigger; "I" statements have the capacity to constructively embrace the leadership moment.

4.   Hold employees responsible for their actions

As a leader there are times when I don't 'nail' a leadership moment, but there is one instance of which I am particularly proud. I had a clinic sister and a senior HR consultant working for me as part of my senior HR management. Both women were exceptionally competent team members, and in my humble opinion, they were both very proficient experts in their fields and had both achieved much. As individuals they were also both good people, however they could not stand each other. They would avoid being in the same room and when they had no choice, such as attending my weekly HR directors meeting, they would both arrive with a tangible 'attitude'.

I *walked past this* a few times and finally reached a level of frustration which left me no choice but to "embrace the moment" and tackle the problem head on. After a particularly unpleasant meeting, where one party had rolled her eyes at the other's proposal, it was obvious to me that the rest of my team was getting irritated. Their irritation was aimed at the two ladies in question certainly, but also at me, for allowing this dynamic to continue unchecked. Enough! I publicly asked them to stay behind after the meeting, which they did.

In my head alarms bells were going off... "Leadership moment! Leadership moment!"

Catching on to what I was lining up, the one said she had an urgent meeting to attend to. I called her bluff and said that, if necessary, I would go to the meeting on her behalf. Then I laid down the rules. I said, *"It appears to me and to the rest of the team that the two of you are allowing your poor relationship to affect our team's performance. I need the members of this team to work in a climate of trust and mutual support. I do not know what your personal issues are, but it needs to stop now. You have a choice. We can sit down and I will play referee and sort this out, or you could sit down yourselves and resolve this like adults. One thing is for certain, you are not leaving this room until this is resolved."*

They chose to resolve the issues themselves and while I know nothing about what was said, I do know there were tears and some shouting. After about two hours they emerged looking as if they had wrestled a wild animal, but it was done and I never had to address this issue with them again! In fact, over time they developed a deep and mature friendship and I seem to recall that one was asked to be a godparent of the other's grandchildren.

While such a positive outcome will not always be the case, the principle take away is that as a leader, *you cannot walk past!* Reflect on what the consequences for everyone would have been if I had continued to ignore this leadership moment and not made these two ladies accountable and responsible for their behaviour and attitudes.

5. **Ensure that everyone is well tasked**

While this seems so logical and easily solved, I am amazed how often this simple management function causes deep-seated friction and frustration.

Lack of role clarity or clear tasking is particularly acute when the responsibility for a very visible activity or project is ambivalent; where a task is the responsibility of more than one person. Remember that sometimes, the cause of the ambivalence may not be obvious to you, and you may believe the exact tasking to be transparent, while in reality it is not.

The best way to check the quality of your tasking is to ask questions. This is resolved relatively easily and reinforces accountability.

Eight tools to positively influence leadership moments

Don't walk past

Focus on the Issue not the person

Hold Responsible for Relationships

Tell Them Why

leadership Moments

Tennis – ball in their court

Help Them Understand

Task Them Well

'I' Statements

This diagram is a useful summary of the moments discussed above and can be used as a quick reference.

How do we become better at leadership moments?

Through reflection and self-awareness. This is the only way that we can grow as leaders.

Have you noticed that there are some people who never seem to learn their lesson? They never seem to respond better to the "big red buttons" in their lives and continuously repeat the same mistakes. This is pretty sad, because as humans we have been given the special ability to learn from our mistakes. Unfortunately, this is not a guaranteed outcome as self-enhancement is dependent on people making conscious decisions to learn and develop. They say wisdom comes with age, but I think that this is only partially true. Wisdom may increase due to experiences, but

> REFLECTION IS THE MOST POWERFUL LEARNING
> TOOL WE HAVE, AND THIS IS PARTICULARLY TRUE WHEN IT COMES TO
> LEARNING ABOUT LEADERSHIP.

I have had the honour to interview several CEOs as part of my research, and one particular interview stands out. This CEO led one of the most significant multinationals in South Africa and was known for his superb leadership style. He focused on developing a corporate leadership brand, so I was not surprised, but rather inspired, when he told me that during his daily commute home, he would ask himself the question: "How did you lead your people today?" He would then spend the next 40 minutes reflecting. It is stirring to imagine just how much a CEO could learn over several years as a consequence of mindful, daily reflection on their individual leadership in action.

> WHEN WE ARE PASSIONATE ABOUT LEADERSHIP, WE REFLECT
> AND LEARN. GETTING INTO THE HABIT OF DOING THIS CAN HAVE
> SIGNIFICANT VALUE AND IS DEFINITELY WORTH INVESTING TIME ON.

Reflection Exercise

Principle 6: Leadership moments amplify the connection/trust experience

Do you understand this concept? Explain.

Does the concept resonate as truth? Why?

Test what is presented against your lived experience.

Reflect upon how you could use this principle in practice.

Chapter 7

Principle 7: Leadership is influence – the product of trust and connection

When a leader has connection and trust with someone, he has influence with that person. Leadership is the ability of one person to influence another person or a group of people towards a common goal. The ability of a leader to influence someone, without using organisational power, is possible, but only if the team member trusts his/her leader. This trust, as we have discussed, flows from how the leader deliberately connected with the team member and how the leader resolved leadership moments. Let's examine this precious facet of leadership influence.

In 2004, Duracell sold Eveready South Africa (ESA), in what Gillette, the listed parent company, believed was a fire sale. As a management team we had totally lost confidence and trust in our previous corporate leaders. Their brutality, lack of vision and high-handed "everything is better in the US" attitude had induced them to sell the company. They had turned a proud, iconic South African company into a struggling local subsidiary of little value.

The sale of ESA turned out to be a godsend. ESA's new owners and the executive team had a distinct plan and a clear vision. I was appointed as ESA's HR Director, and this initiated an incredible 10-year period in my life. I had total freedom to do what I do best. I was the person accountable for all matters HR. There was no head office in the USA or heavy-handed shareholders to contend with.

We were building a new company and we were full of hope and passion. We were all about doing something outstanding; something that would give us an opportunity to create an organisation which looked and functioned differently to anything any of us had experienced in the corporate world before. While this was still a business at core, it was fun, there was flow, and it was incredibly empowering.

What made the difference for me, was the passion and energy of our new MD.

Our new MD was different; he was 100% committed and he pushed hard. What made the difference? He was brutally honest, he really worked on building very close relationships, he communicated a strong vision, he took a keen interest in getting to know his team, and he trusted us. He had confidence that his team would practice good judgement and that we would be completely transparent and proactive when things went wrong.

Because of his style of leadership and influence, the ESA leadership team became maverick and agile. We followed him spontaneously. We did not need to check in for key decisions; we knew what he wanted and we expedited his expectations swiftly. When we succeeded, we celebrated! This was the first time in my life I felt the power of real leadership influence. I experienced a gentle but insistent inspiration which emerges from a deep value system and a clear vision, built squarely on trust and great relationship-based leadership.

This is where I experienced and understood that *influence,* the source of leadership, flows from trust, and trust from connection.

As we have already explored in the preceding four principles, trust, trust and more trust in a leader is in essence what the followers experience when their leader truly connects with them. In simple terms, I learn to trust my leader based on how he/she conducts him/herself when engaging/connecting with me.

If you, as my leader, demonstrate an investment in our relationship, and if I discover that you, as my leader, are capable (know what you are doing) and consistent, then over time I will learn to trust you.

With trust such as this, the magic of real modern relationship-based leadership becomes possible.

What am I talking about? I am talking about the power of influence. This is a simple principle.

> "WHEN I TRUST YOU, MY LEADER, I GIVE YOU THE
> PRICELESS GIFT OF INFLUENCE."

Think about it. If I ask you to do something which runs counter to your instinct, would you do it? Probably not, unless I hold some degree of power over you and am able to force your obedience or compliance, or you have submitted unwillingly to my strength of influence over you. You will only grant me this treasure (carrying out my direction) if you really trust me.

CONNECTION BUILDS TRUST, AND TRUST IS THE FOUNDATION OF
LEADERSHIP INFLUENCE.

I offer this simple linear insight as to how leadership functions in a modern organisation. It is noteworthy that this clear and basic understanding is well supported in literature on the subject.

Take note of a few examples of what the experts say about leadership and influence. There are literally hundreds of different definitions of leadership, each one opening a little facet of one of life's most significant concepts. Many of them contain the term "influence imbedded".

> Peter Northouse, perhaps one of the most prolific business school writers:
> *"Leadership – a process whereby an individual influences a group of individuals to achieve a common goal."*

> John Maxwell, the leadership mega bestseller:
> *"Leadership is Influence – nothing more nothing less."*

> Bernard Bass, father of transformational leadership:
> *"The extent to which a leader is transformational, is measured first, in terms of his/her influence on the followers."*

> Simon Sinek, author and TED bestseller:
> *"Being a leader requires having people that choose to follow you. (Influence)."*

Trust must be established before any person willingly makes the decision to follow you; it is a concrete feeling that begins to emerge when we have a sense that another person or organisation is driven by motives other than their own self-gain. We have to earn trust by communicating and demonstrating that we share the same values and beliefs that will benefit our followers.

These and numerous other leadership gurus have described leadership in different terms, but on reflection, when we talk about the leadership relationship (in the transformational leadership context), as we have already established, the connected/engaged relationship must exist for the relationship to exert influence. How else could I lead effectively?

While the idea of one person influencing another may sound a little as though the follower is somehow being manipulated, this is not the case when influence flows from trust, i.e., trust founded upon my experience of your commitment to me.

TRUST BASED INFLUENCE – THE MAGIC INGREDIENT.

What happens when a leadership relationship emerges that is based on trust?

Neuroscience is currently helping us to understand our human response to one another with much more clarity than ever before in the history of human existence. This is as true in the leadership world as in other areas of human study.

We now know that our frontal lobe is the processor of the brain; this is where our thoughts accumulate and where we bring together our understanding of the outside world from our knowledge and experience. This is the part of our intellect which generates creativity and problem solving. It is the part of the brain that we, as leaders, really need to switch on, i.e., we need our people to be operating primarily in this domain.

This is the mental domain where creativity and innovation emerge, where competitive advantage is envisaged and created. We also know that our frontal cortex only really functions when we are in a trusted state.

The alternative is our medulla, or primitive brain. This is the part of the brain that is designed for survival by responding to the "fight or flight" reflex, and which drives our behaviours and relationships. This part of the brain remains dormant when we are in a relaxed, non-threatened or trusting state, yet this amazing part of our anatomy activates when we feel threatened. When our ancestors encountered the sabre-toothed tiger while hunting for food, the instinctive brain triggered, flooding the body with adrenalin and cortisol. In this state we operate almost instinctively to protect ourselves. This is the mental state best used in combat – not thinking, but rather reacting. This mental state dominates our thinking patterns when our team members are responding to or experience fear.

The trust-based leader, feeds the dynamic nature of their team members frontal cortex, and thus achieve results which over time will far out shine a fear based culture. I am referring expressly to a progressive and transformative trust-based leadership relationship. Here I am talking about that positive energy which is made possible when a trusted leader, who is passionate about the follower's growth and best self, influences him/her towards a common goal; a goal which both parties understand embody at the very least, a mutually beneficial outcome.

Returning to the principle, leadership as a choice, which we discussed in Chapter 1, the choice to build leadership relationships through deliberate connection, building trust and thus acquiring influence, takes focus, commitment, time and effort from the leader. The return on this effort, however, is that we experience the team member at their most productive, creative and inspired. This sequence is illustrated below:

Influence

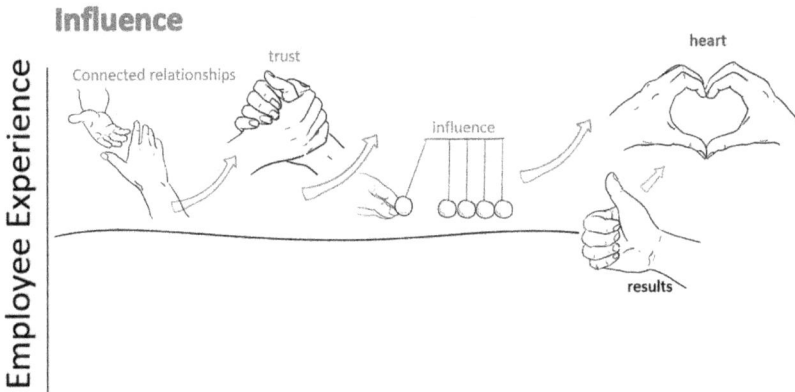

Sadly, the experiences of team members across corporate and social leadership reveal that many leaders do not make this choice, or do not lead from a position of deliberate intent. In the next chapter we will look at the alternative extreme approach.

Reflection Exercise

Principle 7: Leadership is influence – the product of trust and connection

Do you understand this concept? Explain in your own words.

Does the concept resonate as truth? Illustrate.

Test what is presented against your lived experience.

Reflect upon how you could apply this truth in practice.

Chapter 8

Principle 8: The alternative to leadership influence is command and fear

"All this warm and fuzzy stuff makes my head spin!" This was a candid response from one of my students, a senior production manager of a large auto manufacturing plant, when he was first confronted with the concepts we have been discussing.

Bear in mind the following concepts as you read this chapter:

- Connecting with others

- Building trust

- Leading with influence

He continued, "The world I live in is a tough environment. This connection thing really isn't my style. If I allow people whom I lead to get too familiar, they're bound to take advantage. Don't you know – familiarity breeds contempt?", he challenged.

I am surprised at how many people have been taught to lead this way, and how many leaders seem to think that this is the best and only way to lead; it is as though they are afraid of simply being human.

If you take some time to reflect on your life, I will guarantee that you will be able to name some bosses who have managed you while at the same time, keeping a 'safe' distance or perhaps even being aloof and inaccessible. The reality is that such leaders often get results, but how did these leaders make you feel and how sustainable were their results over time?

So why would we want to focus on this soft, fuzzy stuff when all we need to do is lead with our positional power?

Firstly, let us explore the adage, "familiarity breeds contempt". This is a very old saying which has its origins in Greek mythology.

This fable was one of Aesop's: "A fox had never seen a lion before, so when she happened to meet the lion for the first time, she all but died of fright. The second time she saw him, she was still afraid, but not as much as before. The third time, the fox was bold enough to go right up to the lion and speak to him."

This fable and the aligned proverb, "familiarity breeds contempt", has been taken out of context by leaders for years. The essence of the fable is that the more we encounter something that we are afraid of, the less we fear it. In a leadership context, this assumes that instilling fear and keeping a distance is what gets the job done – if you get too close to or connect more personally with your subordinates they will no longer fear or respect you and you will not be able to direct and control the outcome effectively.

This may appear to make sense – that we lead by using the positional power we have been granted when we take on a title or position. Because I am your manager, you will respect me, or, I don't care if you respect me, but you are obliged to respect my position.

Back to my production manager friend. A day later and after considering the alternatives to leading through building trust and influence, he was a convert. In fact, I am convinced that he had been leading instinctively through influence but had never really been aware that he was doing so.

So how does leading through positional power work?

When we lead this way, we are leading from the strength of our position, *not through influence*. Employees will respond, but their responses will be based on fear and command.

When someone commands you to do something, this is the inference: *"I'm not interested in your views. If you can't do it, tell me and I will find someone else who can."* In response we react with fear, or we are offended. Either way, ultimately it is fear that will drive our behaviour.

As opposed to trust, fear is grounded in distrust: fear that my leader will not have my best interests at heart; that I will be embarrassed by my leader; that he/she possesses a hidden agenda and that I only see part of the picture; that if I cross my leader, I will be disadvantaged; that if I do not comply, my best interests and intentions will be undermined. This fear can be disabling and disruptive; it holds us back and handicaps us.

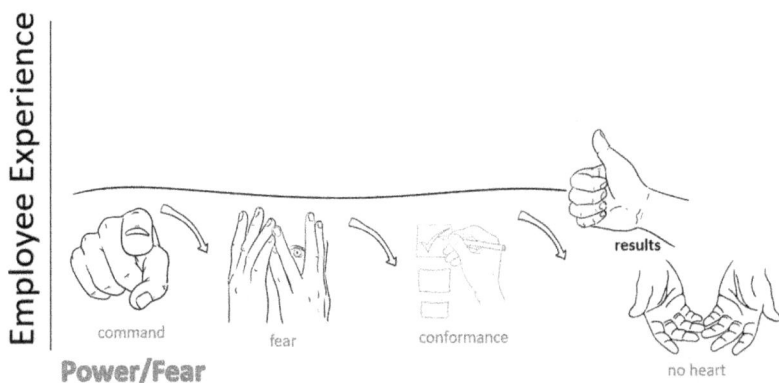

We generally respond to fear either by doing nothing more than the minimum required or even doing the task well, not because we respect or care about our leader but because we are self-motivated. In such a context, we are motivated to ensure that we *survive* rather than *thrive*. Energy that would be better expended on performing is wasted on venting and complaining to one another, and on figuring out ways in which we can self-protect.

In one of the organisations I worked for we had this crude description of the company dynamic: "The senior monkey sitting at the top of the tree looks down and sees smiling faces. The monkeys looking up the tree have a vastly different view."

Unfortunately, the reality is that leaders who rule with fear demand compliance, and will often get results, sometimes even spectacular results. So why not go this route? Why would we bother with relationships and trust-based leadership?

Think about this...

COMPLIANCE MAY LOOK LIKE INFLUENCE, AND THE SHORT-TERM RESULTS MAY LOOK THE SAME, BUT THESE ARE TWO VERY DIFFERENT LEADERSHIP RELATIONSHIPS AND OVER TIME WILL PRODUCE TWO VERY DIFFERENT RESPONSES FROM SUBORDINATES.

When we said at the beginning of the book that "leadership is a choice", this is the choice we were referring to – the choice to build trusted relationships with our people and consequently to lead with positive influence, or to use our positional power to achieve compliance, essentially through instilling fear.

The diagram below depicts how this choice evolves.

The Leadership Choice

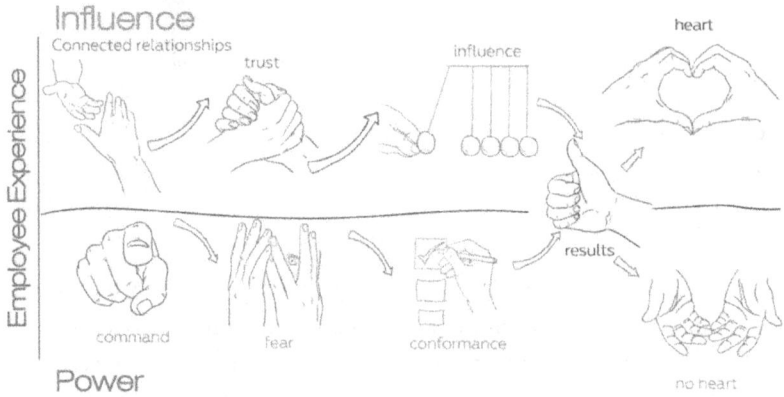

The diagram shows that we have a choice, which is to connect deliberately, instil a level of trust and then lead with influence, or alternatively, based upon our positional power, use the command, fear and compliance style.

In reality, with the exception of the totally absent or abdicated leader, every leader displays some level of both the extreme examples illustrated above. The question is: "What is your dominant style?"

To illustrate: In the case where an influential (top line) leader encounters a situation where he or she needs immediate compliance, the team member, knowing that the leader does not employ command, fear and compliance tactics as a usual approach, would be unlikely to resist the urgent direction given by the leader. The team member would be able to quickly identify the need for the team to respond unwaveringly to the instruction.

The leader who normally takes the command approach as his/her dominant style will perhaps not get the same positive reaction (willingness to co-operate swiftly) as their urgent command is likely to sound like business as usual to the team member.

Reflection Exercise

Principle 8: The alternative to leadership influence is command and fear

Look at the diagram on page 71. Can you, in your personal experience, identify examples of leaders who practiced both the blue and red approaches to leadership?

Which style would you say best describes the leader who has had the most profound positive influence upon your life?

Which style would you say best describes your leadership style? Why?

Chapter 9

Principle 9: An organisation's culture is the reflection of the organisation's leadership

I spent one miserable year working for a large Southern European company. One of the perks of being a manager here was having access to the executive gym, which all the senior management team used. While it was furnished with only a few pieces of equipment, they were state-of-the-art and offered an opportunity for us to exercise directly before or after work without the schlepp of driving to another gym.

The gym facilities were also utilised by my Southern European boss, the Country Manager. He had clearly been trained in an outdated, almost 'mafia style' leadership tradition. He ardently held the belief that "familiarity breeds contempt". He vocalised this often and practiced it strictly. He made no attempt to develop relationships with his senior team and kept us all at arm's length. He was so committed to keeping his distance that he avoided training in the gym at the same time as me. If he happened to come in while I was there, he would avoid eye contact or making conversation.

This was incredibly disheartening to experience in a modern company such as this. While we spent many hours working together our relationship was kept at a superficial distance. We never ate together, never had team functions, never got to know anything more about each other than the bare minimum. Did I learn to trust him? Not at all; I learnt to avoid him at all costs. Work was miserable and everyone was simply in survival mode. The meagre moments of humanity were so inauthentic that they resulted in a 'yes' culture. Everything that he said was to be accepted as truth and every opinion of his agreed with vigorously.

Because of this disconnected attitude and the way in which he operated, everyone distrusted not only our mafia style boss, but somehow by extension we were influenced to distrust one another.

The dominant culture in this company was one of fear and politics between employees and departments, which was distressing. People spoke behind one another's backs and undermined others for their own benefit. There was so little trust that every expense had to be signed off with the CFO's signature, which gave the CFO, who was a clone of the MD, disproportionate power in the organisation.

The company produced a very simple volume product so there seemed to be scant need for applying the potential superpowers that a different culture would have released. We produced the necessary results, and the shareholders were kept happy.

Despite our performance levels, there were fundamental flaws in the organisation, however. During my brief time in this company, I was required to launch a new product. The budgeting of this process, which could have taken a week, took months of indecision and back and forth double checking. We had to renegotiate deadlines and completely took our eyes off the daily operations. Much screaming and shouting and negative energy ensued!

Young talent in our company quickly picked up that this was an unhealthy environment and there was little investment in them as employees from a human standpoint. At one point I was aware that all the members of the senior management team were pursuing alternative employment options. We achieved short-term results, but we had no opportunities to truly progress. The reality was that there was no soul, no heart, no commitment, no creativity and no agility. The lack of familiarity seemed to breed something much more corrosive than contempt – it bred a culture of fear and disengagement!

Why is culture so important?

You may think that superior products, strategy, or people are the differentiators between terrific and average companies, and this could be true in the short-term. However, there is a differentiator which cannot be 'copied and pasted' and cannot be purchased 'off-the-shelf' as it were, and that is an organisation's *culture*.

A high-performance work culture: The organisational Holy Grail

All companies possess latent potential. They have the capacity for employees to:

- fully utilise their talents;
- be free to create and experiment;
- focus on producing excellent value for their customers;

- trust each other and collaborate for a greater purpose; and

- behave in an agile and flexible way.

This is what could be called a high-performance company culture; a trust-based environment that delivers at an optimal level. Unfortunately, this is seldom fully realised.

Striving for this ideal would provide a massive opportunity for competitive advantage. This is the standard against which employee engagement surveys measure organisational culture.

A fractured organisation

I was searching for an antonym to illustrate what the opposite of a high-performance culture is, when the South African president, Cyril Ramaphosa, nailed it for me. Directly after his dethroning of Jacob Zuma, he addressed the World Trade Organisation and described the ANC as, *"a fractured organisation".*

He added that: "We, in South Africa, know what a fractured world is. We come from a fractured country and a fractured past, which was fractured by the past policies of apartheid and has resulted in the poverty, inequality, and unemployment that we face today.... The first thing that I think all of us as South Africans have acknowledged is that we are living in a country which has a fractured past, a currently fractured present and therefore, it falls on all of us to do something about this."

So, on the other end of the spectrum from a high-performance culture, lies a fractured organisational culture.

This is a culture where the dominant driving force is *fear*; where employees behave in the opposite way to that which presents in a high-performance culture.

In a fractured organisational culture:

- people do as they are told;

- people are afraid to do anything that is out of the ordinary;

- the focus is on self-protection;

- people are political and fear each other, creating silos and "in" and "out" groups; and

- climate change is difficult and often scary.

Why do different organisational cultures emerge?

By definition, a leadership culture is the collective leadership experience that subordinates encounter over time. When employees are sitting in the canteen or talking at a coffee station, and one employee says to another, *"You'll never guess what they've done now!"*, the "they" referred to is the collective leadership. Starting with executive leadership, a leadership culture emerges progressively due to the way an organisation leads and what their dominant form of leadership culture embodies.

While organisational culture is a complex dynamic, I have become convinced that it is the shadow of the dominant leadership culture. In other words, the tone or organisational culture is set by its leadership.

The way in which leaders connect, build trust and gain influence will determine the extent to which a high-performance leadership culture could emerge. The reason for this is that in an environment of trust, people perform optimally – they are free to focus on their purpose, to experiment and to suggest new approaches. They are happier to accept changes without being overly concerned because their best interests are secure.

Conversely, the extent to which leaders achieve results by fear and resultant compliance (command-based leadership) will determine just how fractured the organisation becomes. This is because when people are responding to fear, they self-protect. To use the language of neuroscience, they Fight, Flight, Freeze or Flee. When people are afraid, they go into survival mode; they begin to politic and form sub-groups of people with the same gripes. The source of their fear drives their behaviour. They shut down their creative minds and focus on themselves and their personal distress. They withhold their individual, potential gift, or skill for influence and simply end up complying. They may even nurture a sense of entitlement regarding their actions and lack 'soul'. This is a fractured organisation!

These different alternatives are illustrated below.

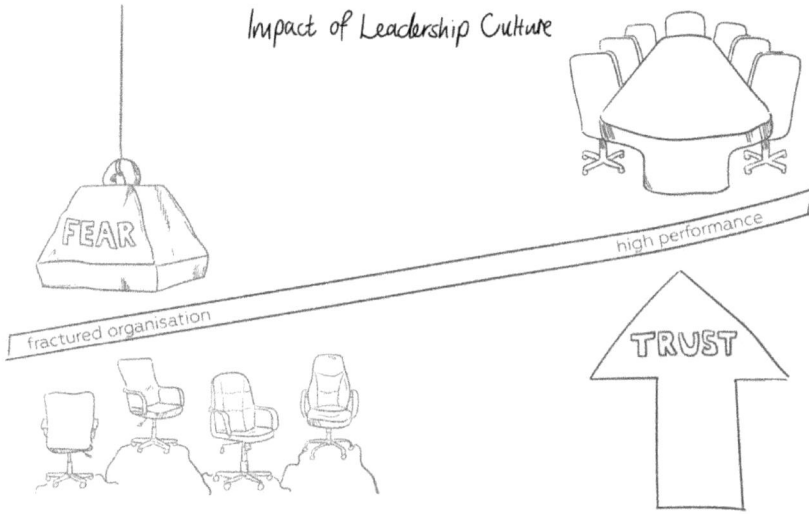

Impact of Leadership Culture

FEAR

fractured organisation

high performance

TRUST

It is interesting to note that leaders who wish to change an organisational culture often invest in communicating the "new culture" to their teams and subordinates, but fail to see how their own behaviour dictates the primary source of culture establishment.

Take a moment to reflect on the stated organisational cultural values below and consider how we respond differently to each, depending on the leadership approach.

Typical value	Follower response when led through fear...	Follower response when led through trust...
Honesty – speak up	I will keep quiet because to speak up is to place myself in the firing line.	I will speak up because you will value this and use my honest input if in the organisation's best interest.
Innovation	Why would I be innovative; the leader knows better? Let him/her figure it out. He will not be interested in what I have to offer.	My leader appreciates my innovation, I am confident that he/she will be open to my ideas.

Typical value	Follower response when led through fear...	Follower response when led through trust...
Teamwork	You must be joking. How can we work as a team if we don't trust each other?	In our team we have each other's backs. I really enjoy being part of this team.
High performance	I will work as hard as I need to avoid the wrath of my leader. I work for my pay.	I will work as hard for this team as I can. No one slacks off as it would put pressure on others in the team. Work is fun!
Integrity	I do what I need to get the job done. Integrity is a good asset, but survival is a better bet.	My leader lives integrity, so it is easy for me to do the same.

Ultimately, the leader sets the tone, and in the case of a leadership team, the collective leadership. This is a significant leadership responsivity. I like to describe it as follows: the culture of an organisation is the shadow of the leader/leadership.

Culture is the shadow of the leader!

Of course, this concept can be challenging to leaders in the middle of an organisation. How do I express a connected trust-based influential leadership approach when my senior managers are not on the same page?

While this question has been posed numerous times in my classes, and every time I have asked, "Let's consider what the alternatives are", I have only ever had four options suggested:

> First, you could leave the department or the company. This is not always a good solution as the grass is not always greener on the other side.

> Second, you could challenge the existing senior leadership, but as the issue is about their choice to practice fear-based leadership, a challenge in this area may be ill-advised.

> Third, you could just comply; be one of them. While this is perhaps the simplest option, it is surely the most unsatisfactory.

Fourth, you could choose to remain authentic to how you wish to lead.

While I cannot guarantee that a poor traditional leader will necessarily accept that you are a modern relationship-based leader, I am convinced that if it is your choice to lead as we have outlined above, you would be best advised to remain authentic. Assuming that you are on top of your game, over time, most often the results of influential leadership will be overwhelmingly positive and senior leadership will shift their focus from input to output. You will also experience that the team members you are privileged to lead will have the potential to perform at their optimum.

This brings us to the end of the nine principles and I sincerely hope that this journey has at the very least started you thinking about what is possible and given you a clear insight as to how to build trust-based relationships deliberately and consciously.

The balance of this book revolves around positioning the approach I have presented in the first nine principles in the context of the development of leadership theory, as well as my view of where leadership thinking will evolve into the future. Before you look at this more theoretical and less applied input, I would like you to use this reflective tool to examine your practical application of leadership:

Reflection Exercise

This reflective exercise is intended to consolidate your thinking around the nine principles presented thus far and to help you to remember them and find ways of applying them.

Principle 1: Leadership is not a 'one-size-fits-all' theory. It is a choice.

Two sides of a coin... Management Leadership	Leadership and management – two sides of the same coin. We manage systems and processes and lead people. Leadership is a choice.
Reflective question: Have you chosen to lead rather than manage?	What does this mean to you in practice?

Principle 2: Leadership is first, a relationship.

performance work culture command **leadership** culture future leadership industrial revolution leadership moment organisational holy grail activation organisation personal experience different organisational culture reflection leadership influence relationship trust experience theory leadership relationship virtual world alternative positional power **connection** title personality type influence leadership brand human relationship predicts of trust statement question **trust** choice	If you choose to lead then it must follow that you have chosen to build trusted relationships.
Reflective question: Are you comfortable with having a leadership relationship with your team members?	

Principle 3: Relationships are about connection and trust.

	Your experience of me elicits a response which is either positive or negative. Over time this response will develop into trust or distrust.
Reflective exercise: Think about a range of people you know both professionally and in your private life. To what extent do you trust/distrust them? Try to rank them in order of trust.	

Principle 4: In a leadership relationship, the leader is responsible for the relationship.

	In a leadership relationship there is accountability. The leader, not the team member, is responsible for building the trust relationship based on the quality of the leader's connection.
Reflective exercise: List the people you are responsible for and assess whether you have no connection, a natural or a strong connection. Use a five-point scale	

Principle 5: Leaders build trust by switching off auto pilot and deliberately connecting.

	We naturally connect to some people based upon our backgrounds, interests or past experiences. As leaders we cannot afford to connect only with some in our team, therefore leadership requires deliberate connection.
Reflective exercise: Think of 10 ways you can deliberately connect with all your team members.	

Principle 6: Leadership moments amplify the connection/trust experience.

	While deliberate connection is the basis of the leadership relationship, there will be leadership moments where our leadership is put to the test. Our response will either enhance or diminish trust.
Reflective exercise: Reflect upon different leadership moments you have encountered and how you could have used tools to improve the outcome.	

Principle 7: Leadership is influence – the product of trust and connection.

Influence / Employee Experience	Leadership means having influence. A leader is someone who can influence a person or group toward a common goal. Influence is the product of trust.
Reflective exercise: Reflect upon a great leader in your past who was able to lead through trust/ connection. What did you learn?	

Principle 8: The alternative to leadership influence is command and fear.

The Leadership Choice / Influence / Employee Experience / Power	The converse of connection, trust and influence is the use of positional power, fear and compliance.
Reflective exercise: Think of a past leader who used positional power to achieve outcomes. Reflect upon how they made you feel and how effective you were under their leadership.	

Principle 9: An organisation's culture reflects the organisation's leadership.

<table>
<tr>
<td>

Impact of Leadership Culture

</td>
<td>

An organisation's culture could be high performance, fractured or somewhere in the middle.

The determining factor is to what extent the organisation is leading through the use of fear as opposed to trust.

</td>
</tr>
<tr>
<td>

Reflective exercise:

Think about your past and current organisation and to what extent the culture was/is high performance or fractured.

To what extent does the leadership of an organisation determine the type of culture?

</td>
<td></td>
</tr>
</table>

PART 2

It is my sincere hope that the journey this book has taken you on thus far has been deeply personal and meaningful for you. I have written Part 1 in a style that is reflective and accessible as it is my hope that you have gained an insight into modern leadership relationships and have a clear idea about how you wish to lead. If so, my purpose in writing this book has been achieved and I wish you the very best on your journey!

Part 2 is somewhat different; I have added this section to give context to the thinking presented in Part 1. The purpose of Part 2 is to allow you, the reader, to have a brief look at how thinking around leadership has evolved and what the future may look like. I trust that you will find it as compelling as I have.

Chapter 10

Summary

Over the past 150 years, society has gone through three Industrial Revolutions and we now stand on the edge of the fourth. As society has progressed through these revolutions, so we have altered both how we see people and as such, how we lead them. When we look at these periods of industrial history from a leadership perspective, two trends emerge. The first trend is that we have increasingly changed how we view the value of our employees and have adjusted our perspective of the impact they have on our organisation's performance and of their importance and contribution to our industries. The second trend is that we have increased our appreciation of the value of our employees and our view on how to lead our team members has shifted.

As the 4th Industrial Revolution comes into full swing as a consequence of, among other drivers, Covid-19, it seems to be clear, in literature at least, that the leadership approach outlined in this book is favoured. Leadership as a relationship, built through connection, trust and influence as opposed to leading through fear, is the future direction. Why do I say this?

Let's briefly take a closer look at each revolution in terms of broad trends, i.e., the value of employees through each revolution, as well as the leadership styles that developed as a result. Over time, what was considered leadership best practice has changed dramatically, and this indicates what the future trends may look like.

Before we look at leadership during the different industrial ages, I would like to make a few somewhat obvious observations.

> First, these revolutions are not date specific and cultures have moved from one to the next in their own time and unique ways.

> Second, many countries and organisations have not yet moved to the third, or even the second, revolution in terms of employee contribution and leadership practice.

> Third, it is possible, although challenging, to be a "modern style" leader in an organisation that has not yet evolved to the next revolution.

The Four Industrial Revolutions

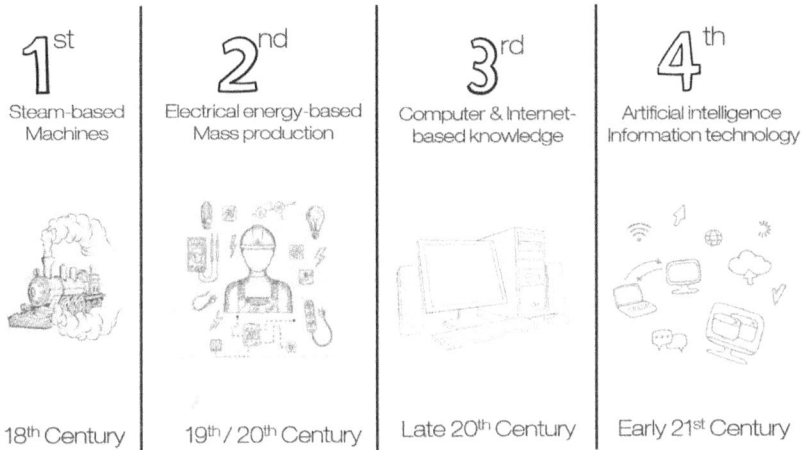

1st	2nd	3rd	4th
Steam-based Machines	Electrical energy-based Mass production	Computer & Internet-based knowledge	Artificial intelligence Information technology
18th Century	19th / 20th Century	Late 20th Century	Early 21st Century

1 The 1st Industrial Revolution

This epic period of history took place over approximately 150 years and began shifting into the 2nd Industrial Revolution just prior to the turn of the 19th century. This was a period of inventions and marked the transition from the craft and artisanal production of resources to that of industrialisation. The use of steam and electricity and the developments of the steam engine in manufacturing, locomotives and steamships were some of the core drivers of this revolution.

Charles Dickens beautifully described how appalling working conditions were during this era. The famous line from the musical rendition of his novel, *Oliver Twist*, which was set during this epoch, perhaps best describes how employees were viewed:

> "One boy, Boy for sale.
> He's going cheap. Only seven guineas. That - or there abouts.
>
> Small boy... Rather pale... Through lack of sleep.
> Feed him gruel dinners. Stop him getting stout.
>
> If I should say he wasn't very greedy... I could not, I'd be telling you a tale.
> One boy, Boy for sale. Come take a peep.
> Have you ever seen as nice a boy for sale?"

This rather sad and moving lyric illustrates how employees were viewed during this period; people were basically reduced to being resources and they were traded as such – a commodity that could be bought or sold. This age saw the Atlantic slave trade from Africa reach its peak. It declined during the Abolition movement which emerged and was implemented across Europe and the Americas from around 1800 to the 1850s.

The bottom line for employees during this period was that in many cases they were seen as little more than a commodity to be traded.

Consequently, the dominant leadership schools of thought were largely aligned to leader-centric thinking.

The term 'Machiavellian' is used by psychologists to describe a callous, manipulative and indifferent personality trait. The term stemmed from the thinking of Niccolò Machiavelli, an Italian political philosopher who advocated that: "As long as the end justifies the means, almost any action by a leader can be justified." During the 1st Industrial Revolution, this was the prevailing approach to leadership.

During this period 'hereditary' leadership was also common, where leadership was bestowed on family members or inherited as a birth right. Leadership was the domain of the elite class. It is evident that at this point in history, leadership had little or nothing to do with ability or relationship-building, and to secure dominance, subordinates were kept subservient and tightly controlled.

Interestingly, when I ask students to identify prevalent leadership traits in modern day society, the 1-IR leadership constructs still seem to be predominant. In South Africa, our apartheid forefathers maintained a hereditary leadership structure through broader industry, and in current political structures there is significant prevalence of patronage and cadre deployment.

This era's dominant leadership practice, as a consequence of viewing the follower as a "commodity/resource", is far removed from the type of leadership we examined in Part 1 of this book.

② The 2nd Industrial Revolution

With the advent of mass production systems, originating with Frederick Taylor in the late 1800s and the early production lines of Henry Ford (1913), industry evolved into the 2nd Industrial Revolution. This period was characterised by the growth of mass production systems, the division of labour and the establishment of modern-day organisational structures of bureaucracy.

As mass production systems grew and flourished, spurred on by two World Wars, management became a recognised business science; we began seeing people as a part of the production process or the means of production. We studied processes, developed roles and recruited people who would fill these roles.

Employee motivation came to be recognised as important, as in many cases these simplified jobs were not intellectually stimulating. The early theories of motivation were developed by a movement called The Behaviourists. Increasingly we understood that money alone was a poor motivator and that the social dynamic of the workplace and being part of a team was crucial.

During this 60-year period in Europe and America, some significant thinking appeared around leadership, especially regarding Frederick Taylor's improved production process. "Dominant Man" theories had been around for some time and are worth looking at. This theory holds that leadership has to do with your presence and personality. We even began testing and assessing for inherent traits that would predict our leadership style.

Towards the latter part of the 2-IR, Hersey and Blanchard published a new leadership theory. Made popular in the book, *Management of Organisational Behaviour*.[3] This Situational Leadership Theory proposed that different types of followers need different leadership styles. A leader from my past, so convinced of the merit of this theory, would present a yearly workshop on this model to the entire leadership team. This philosophy argues that the leader adjusts his or her leadership style dependent on the maturity and ability of the follower.

Telling	Selling	Participating	Delegating
Individuals lack the specific skills required for the job in hand, but they are willing to work at the task. They are novices but enthusiastic.	Individuals are more capable of fulfilling the task, however they are demotivated and unwilling to do it.	Individuals are experienced and capable of doing the task but lack the confidence or willingness to take on the responsibility.	Individuals are experienced at the task and comfortable with their own ability to do it well. They are able and willing to not only do the task, but to take responsibility for it.

Blake and Mouton presented the managerial grid below:

Leadership style	Concern for people	Concern for production
Laissez faire	Low	Low
Country club	High	Low
Authority-compliance	Low	High
Team	High	High

These theories affected two dimensions. First, they recognised that leading well and appropriately made a marked difference, and second, they recognised that employees made a difference.

In 1960, towards the end of the 2-IR, McGregor published his "X, Y" theory which basically drew a line in the sand.[4] Managers fell into one of two camps based upon their view of the employee:

Theory X: employees were judged to be innately lazy and lacking in enthusiasm to contribute, and therefore needed heavy-handed leadership.

Theory Y: employees needed to feel part of something meaningful and be given the room to contribute to that purpose, and could produce spectacular results if well led.

As we increasingly understood that employees were a key 'tool' or a means of getting things done productively, we evolved theories which focused on what leaders 'did' as opposed to 'who they were'.

Reflecting back on Part 1 for this book, we see the shift in direction already starting to emerge. During this period, the "other side of the coin", i.e., the professional manager with detailed skill sets, came into the forefront of business science as a field and leadership continued to evolve towards a greater recognition of the value of the follower.

③ The 3rd Industrial Revolution

From the late 1960s until recently, we have been riding a rollercoaster! The speed of development and transitions are unprecedented in the history of mankind. This age is called the 'Information Age'.

Two personal observations illustrate this massive change. I can still clearly remember the trauma my parents went through every time an encyclopaedia salesman would pay a visit. My parents were left with the sense that by not investing their life savings into this expensive wall of books, they were depriving us kids of any chance of gaining knowledge. Ironically, you can still purchase untouched Encyclopaedia Britannica series in second-hand charity stores!

Now if my teenage son wants to know anything, from the latest FIFA result to quantum physics, all he does is say, "Hey Siri", and the answer is available from the best current sources globally.

In my youth, when I spent three months in Germany, I made a Hungarian friend. Despite language difficulties, we travelled and did cool stuff together. When I returned home, I promised I would keep in touch. I did the only thing I could at the time, I wrote letters. By contrast, I recently watched my son play an online game called "Fortnight" with a group of friends. They were collaborating in a small fighting group and were guiding and protecting each other against other competitors. It is remarkable that these best mates could communicate with each other in real-time, despite being separated geographically by entire continents, ranging from the UK to Australia, Korea and South Africa.

The world has shifted dramatically over my lifetime, and with it has come the realisation that the employee is a vitally important component of any company. It has now become commonplace for CEOs to rattle off the clichéd saying, *"Our people are our greatest assets".*

We hand-pick skills and pay extra to retain employees we value. We pay bonuses in recognition of performance, and we support their growth when budget allows.

For all this, of course, we demand performance.

We have, in fact, become so focused on deriving value from our human assets that we take a similar approach to them as we do towards our financial assets. If I consider the extent of the KPIs, performance management systems, objectives and other reporting requirements now, as opposed to my early professional life, the change has been drastic.

WE NOW VIEW HUMAN ASSETS AND PHYSICAL ASSETS SIMILARLY.

"WE SWEAT THEM, MEASURE THEM, CONTROL THEM AND OVER TIME DEPRECIATE THEM."

From a leadership perspective, there is an appreciation, theoretically at least, that if our people are well led, they will perform well.

Our approach to leading our human assets has matured and altered from the approaches prevalent in both the 1-IR and 2-IR. How we lead is substantially more focused on the role of the leader!

The earliest leadership theory to gain support in the emerging digital age was named 'Transactional Leadership' or 'LMX leadership' (Leadership Member Exchange). This approach views leadership as precisely that, a transaction. If the leader needs to get something done, he or she uses incentive or punishment as two alternative approaches. A transaction, for instance, would sound something like this: "I am good to you, I provide you with a great facility and benefits, and thus, I expect you to be loyal to me." Transactional leadership largely uses what we call *extrinsic rewards.*

This is a rather basic form of relationship and with the passing of time, transactional leadership was replaced in the mid-1980s with transformational leadership. Transformational leadership focuses on influence and intrinsic motivation (from within). Transformational leaders are aware of and celebrate the potential of each follower – they inspire, empower and motivate followers to reach unanticipated performance levels. Transformational leaders invest in the well-being of their followers.

There are four commonly recognised components to transformational leadership, sometimes referred to as the 4 Is:

- **Idealised influence**: walking the talk and actively leading through inspiration and influence.

- **Inspirational motivation**: using intrinsic motivation through the clear articulation of a strategy or vision.

- **Individual consideration**: a genuine care and investment in the well-being and growth of the individual.

- **Intellectual stimulation**: challenging higher levels of performance and innovation. Leading in the 1990s: The Four I's of Transformational Leadership.[5]

- While the more than 30-year-old transformational leadership theory is still pervasive today, its framework comfortably accommodates the nine principles we have referred to in this book.

The leadership book industry has boomed over the past 20 years, with numerous significant ideas emerging. Most of these theories have moved from the charismatic ideal of a leadership position to *how* leaders influence followers and create richness in their lives. We will very briefly touch on some of these concepts.

Servant leadership: the idea that the leader takes the subordinate's success to heart and sees the role of leader as being one of service to the follower, as opposed to overseeing.

Positive psychology: the idea that the modern leader shifts focus from criticising what went wrong to looking for any positive contribution and celebrating it.

Organic leadership: where the leadership paradigm has altered the notions of traditional leadership paradigms.[6] New leadership models are geared towards a more relational process and a shared or distributed experience, which can occur at different levels depending on social interactions and networks of influence.[7]

The law of the lid: of the 21 laws of leadership presented by John Maxwell, I like the law of the lid most. It is a principal that acknowledges that an organisation's performance will be constrained by the "lid" or the level at which leaders allow followers to perform.

Authentic leadership: this is thinking which has emerged, to some degree, due to the disparity within leadership that has been so pervasive in society. Authentic leadership is reflective and grounded; it is genuine, self-aware and transparent. This authenticity inspires loyalty and trust.

Summary

We are adjusting how we view employees as well as how we decide which leadership theory is appropriate.

Thinking has shifted in terms of how employees have been viewed as well as deciding which leadership theory is appropriate.

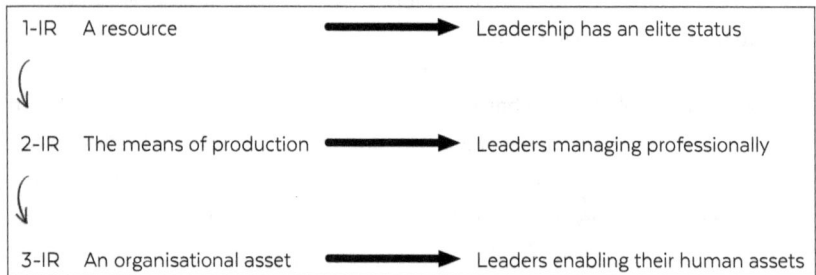

1-IR	A resource	⟶ Leadership has an elite status
2-IR	The means of production	⟶ Leaders managing professionally
3-IR	An organisational asset	⟶ Leaders enabling their human assets

Chapter 11

Future leadership – leading in a virtual world

At time of writing, , huge office blocks stand unused, and our people are working from home on endless Zoom meetings, cursing bandwidth issues and often lacking basic tools, such as two monitor screens and a comfortable office chair. AI, machine learning, block chain and big data are facilitating our navigation of the complexities of a world that is significantly altered. Covid 19 has plunged us ito the 4th Industrial revolution.

I have spent a great deal of time brainstorming the question, 'What will leadership look like in the 4th IR?' What are the main drivers that will determine how we will view our subordinates in the 4th Industrial Revolution, and what will the impact of this be on how we view leadership?

The 4th Industrial Revolution will inevitably result in technology increasingly replacing human activities. Some are of the opinion that people will therefore become less important and that leadership styles will reflect this shift. I believe that this is unlikely, and that the natural trend is diametrically opposed to this view. Allow me to share my reasons.

Looking into the future it is often useful to reflect upon what is driving any change. Let's examine some of the drivers that may impact upon future employee and leadership trends.

1. **Shift to diversity**: as we transition to the new world, it is increasingly apparent that significant advantages lie in divergent insights. Creating a diverse workplace is progressively being understood as more than just the right thing to do; rather it is an absolute necessity of competitiveness. The wider the spread of ideas and insight, the more responsive an organisation will have to be to complex global markets. Leading at this level places significant strain on the existing 'old school' leadership; it is not simply a matter of including people from diverse backgrounds, it is the insight that, in variation of thought lies the competitive difference and advantage.

2. **The combination of artificial intelligence, machine learning, big data, block chain, crypto currency, 3-D printing, and a plethora of new technological**

developments emerging: the interface between all these developments is changing the world as we know it. These developments will have a profound impact on people and how organisations function.

a.   In the technological arena our capability to leverage this new technology is critical. The equipment itself will be available to anyone with the necessary capital. The differentiator will be in how well we are able to leverage the possibilities they offer and our ability to integrate the relevant equipment across platforms and processes. Leveraging these new opportunities requires nothing less than people – people who are empowered and creative and who are inspired and thriving in the new world.

b.   The great divide – the disparity between the "haves" and "have nots" – will expand. Consider this... if you have a smartphone, you are privileged. You have instant access to the world's greatest encyclopaedia where all possible knowledge is available. You live in the new world.

If you do not, you are unlikely to ever own one. Financial status distinguishes between people who have transitioned into IR4 and those who are trapped in the old world. While this divide has always been there, it will become more acute, and society's ability to improve the quality of life for those on the fringes will become more difficult. These challenges will play out in our future society and will place huge demands on future leaders.

3.   **New skills**: This new world will embrace a whole new skills set. The World Economic Forum recently stated that 65% of children entering primary school today will ultimately end up working in completely new job types that don't yet exist.[8] Organisations will be searching for skills that are not currently available, and at the same time, it is well documented that other skills will become irrelevant.

People with modern skills sets could potentially become traded currency, much like the football stars of the contemporary game. There is no reason to believe that the war for skills, which has raged globally for the past decade, will in any way dissipate.

In this context we know that people more often leave and resign from managers than from companies, and thus productive leadership brands will become crucial currency.

4. **A new level of autonomy**: along with these new skills, leaders will need to allow a new level of autonomy which was not projected during the 2nd, and to some degree the 3rd, Industrial Revolution. You have spent a significant amount of time in your career developing a skill set, however the chances and reality are that unless you are making a conscious effort to keep abreast of your field, if you graduated five years or more ago, you are already considerably behind developments.

This will require leaders who are comfortable leading people who are more skilled than themselves.

5. **New freedoms**: Black Lives Matter, the Me Too movement, the rise of Conservatism, a Voice for the Youth. These movements and the speed at which information is available means that injustice and discrimination practices are immediately exposed. In South Africa we have seen innumerable such exposures, from the H&M 'Monkey' shirt debacle to Trésemme's Hair Products being slammed for racist marketing.

In years past, many successful leaders were robust and outspoken; they did not restrain themselves and would expound the truth as they saw it. This has changed significantly. People not speaking out if they are mistreated and exhibiting blind compliance will be viewed as a betrayal and compromise of self. The workplace has seen a far greater consciousness of human rights' boundaries and modern leadership needs to reflect a far greater respect for individual rights across the politically correct spectrum.

6. **A shrinking globe**: we live in a world where travel across borders is commonplace and maintaining global connections is part of everyday life. We can provide training remotely across continents and share the best ideas in a heartbeat. Our shipping lanes are congested with products moving between East and West. We are purchasing Chinese ingredients in Africa, and there is a Nando's fast-food chain in London. We order products online from anywhere in the world and chat to local and international partners on Zoom and MS Teams.

Having lived through Covid-19, however, we have been thrust into a world where our very existence is dependent on our digital online presence; where our only means of connection is to reach out and connect via online and remote tools and platforms.

7. **Improved work life balance and remote work**: the Covid-19 pandemic dramatically altered everyone's thinking in this regard. The challenge of leading remote teams is no longer a theoretical debate, but our lived experience. Does this mean that leaders can relax about their relationships with their reports as they will seldom see them face-to-face? Not even slightly! On the contrary, the conversation we took for granted at the water fountain must now evolve into a deliberate act. How well we help our staff connect and feel part of an organisation will become a competitive advantage issue.

8. **Speed**: Need I say more? Pace will become everything, and this will directly impact on our ability to lead. Gone are the days where a leader can afford to hold up a decision to exercise and demonstrate some ego-driven level of status. Leaders who can create enabling environments will themselves thrive, and the leaders who view their position as some form of special privilege may find that they are quickly exposed.

9. **The future generations**: so much has been said about Millennials, but to be honest, we are seeing a series of new generational shifts, where technology and the world of digital communication, social media and a host of other tools have become second nature to these future generations. The shift in technology, as well as the shift in authority structures, means that these very skilled young people are upfront about their leaders and their experiences. They will not wait for things to get better or suck up any unwarranted heavy handedness – they will disengage, or they will leave. They expect life balance, and they expect to be well led.

The above direction indicators are just a selection of some of the signboards around future leadership in a new world, which could be indicating one of two directions:

We could be facing a world where people are less important and consequently where leadership is a non-issue, or we could be facing a world where people, and our ability to inspire them and create a thriving environment and culture, are the arena of future competitiveness. In this scenario, leadership will become an even more critical skill for those who are able to build trust and influence the future heroes of organisations and our world.

Conclusion

Each of these drivers highlight an increased need for people to be recognised at the human and relationship levels. They emphasise the importance of relationships and the need for increased trust between team members and leaders, and they show just how important the human superpowers we discussed in Chapter 9 have become. Will our leadership relationships be more or less important in the future? I am convinced that they will be more crucial than ever.

In my programmes on leadership, I love to ask this question: "If each of us in this class were given six robots, would we produce the exact same quality and sell the same volumes?" Surely not. Why the disparity? Clearly the different outcomes would reflect individuality and people's divergent capabilities.

This is perhaps self-evident, but I then ask the class to stay with me and take the argument further. Imagine that there are two companies competing with each other in a very cut-throat market, and let's assume that by chance each company has the same access to capital, equipment, resources and skills. Would these companies as a consequence produce to the same quality and sell the same volumes? Most often when I ask this question one or two people would agree that they would, but the balance of the class would wrestle with the question further.

Then I ask, "Imagine if the one company was under the leadership of someone who deliberately connected with team members, who in turn trusted that the leader was very capable, cared about the team members' best interests and was consistent? And the other company was led by an ego-driven leader who preferred to lord it over his followers who worked in a constant state of fear. Would these companies still produce to the same quality and sell the same volumes?"

This always sparks debate. Not about which company would perform better in the long run, as the influential leader's company performance is a no brainer. The debate is usually whether the leader who enforces compliance might be able to compete in the short term.

I am convinced that leadership choices make the difference and that great leaders have the potential to create environments where team members thrive and where high performance is the consequence. I am further convinced that such leadership is entirely possible in each of us.

What will make the difference is whether as a leader we consciously choose to build trusted relationships, and as a consequence achieve influence or not. The choice is simple, the art lies in the consistent practice of this kind of leadership.

Success lies in constant reflection and adjustment. This is not unattainable nor is it wildly complicated, but it does require significant dedication to a passion for people.

In conclusion, I truly hope you have enjoyed and benefited personally from this journey with me, and I wish you well on your path to *being* that leader who will have the cherished gift of your team's trust and that you will be a source of inspiration to them!

Additional Reading

Anthony, L. (2009). *The Elephant Whisperer: The Extraordinary Story of One Man's Battle to Save His Herd.* , New York: Pam MacMillan.

Du Toit. C. (2016). *The new leadership landscape.* In L. Van der Merwe., & A. Verwey. (2016) *Building The Corporate Leadership Community: Creating a common purpose for and shared meaning of organisational leadership.* Randburg: Knowledge Resources.

Folkman, Z. (2022). *Understanding the Trifecta of Trust.* Available from: https://www.youtube.com/watch?app=desktop&v=DFLUg3T-AFw

Lencioni, P. (2002). *The five dysfunctions of as team: A leadership fable.* San Francisco: Jossey Bass.

McKeown, G. & Wizeman, L. (2010). *Multipliers: How the Best Leaders Make Everyone Smarter.* New York: HarperCollins.

Schieber, P. (1987), The wit and wisdom of Grace Hopper'. *The OCLC Newsletter 167,* n.p. Available from: http://www.cs.yale.edu/homes/tap/Files/hopper-wit.html

Toor, S., & Ofori, G. (2008). Leadership versus Management: How They Are Different, and Why. *Leadership and Management in Engineering, 8*(2). DOI:10.1061/(ASCE)1532-6748(2008)8:2(61).

Zenger, J., Folkman, J., Sherwin, R., & Steel, B. (2012). *How to Be Exceptional: Drive Leadership Success By Magnifying Your Strengths.* New York: McGraw Hill.

Endnotes

1   Du Toit, C. (2017). *The Immeasurable Value of Discovering Your 'Personal Leadership Brand'*. Retrieved from: https://charlesdutoit.co.za/2017/12/09/the-immeasurable-value-of-discovering-your-personal-leadership-brand/

2   Folkman, Z. (2019). *The Trifecta of Trust*. Available from: https://zengerfolkman.com/the-trifecta-of-trust/

3   Hersey, P., & Blanchard, K.H. (1969). *Management of Organizational Behavior: Utilizing Human Resources*. New Jersey: Prentice Hall.

4   McGregor, D.M. (1960). *The Human Side of Enterprise*. New York: McGraw-Hill.

5   Avolio, B. J., Waldman, D. A., & Yammarino, F. J. (1991). Leading in the 1990s: The Four I's of Transformational Leadership. *Journal of European Industrial Training, 15*(4): 9-16. https://doi.org/10.1108/03090599110143366

6   Avery, G.C. (2004). *Understanding Leadership: Paradigms and Cases*. London: Sage

7   Fletcher, J.K., & Kaufer, K. (2003). *Shared leadership*. In C.L. Pearce & J.A. Conger (Eds.), *Shared leadership: Reframing the hows and whys of leadership*. Thousand Oaks, California: Sage.

8   World Economic Forum. 2016. *The Future of Jobs: Employment, Skills and Workforce Strategy for the Fourth Industrial Revolution*. Available from: https://www3.weforum.org/docs/WEF_FOJ_Executive_Summary_Jobs.pdf

Index

www.ingramcontent.com/pod-product-compliance
Lightning Source LLC
Chambersburg PA
CBHW071214200326
41519CB00018B/5514